Lean Startups
for Social Change

Lean Startups for Social Change

The Revolutionary Path to Big Impact

MICHEL GELOBTER

Foreword by Steve Blank

Introduction by Christie George

BK

Berrett–Koehler Publishers, Inc.
a BK Currents book

Berrett-Koehler Publishers, Inc.
1333 Broadway, Suite 1000
Oakland, CA 94612-1921
Tel: (510) 817-2277   Fax: (510) 817-2278   www.bkconnection.com

Ordering Information
Quantity sales. Special discounts are available on quantity purchases by corporations, associations, and others. For details, contact the "Special Sales Department" at the Berrett-Koehler address above.
Individual sales. Berrett-Koehler publications are available through most bookstores. They can also be ordered directly from Berrett-Koehler: Tel: (800) 929-2929; Fax: (802) 864-7626; www. bkconnection.com
Orders for college textbook/course adoption use. Please contact Berrett-Koehler: Tel: (800) 929-2929; Fax: (802) 864-7626.
Orders by U.S. trade bookstores and wholesalers. Please contact Ingram Publisher Services:` Tel: (800) 509-4887; Fax: (800) 838-1149; E-mail: customer.service@ingrampublisherservices.com; or visit www.ingrampublisherservices.com/Ordering for details about electronic ordering.

Berrett-Koehler and the BK logo are registered trademarks of Berrett-Koehler Publishers, Inc.

Printed in the United States of America

Berrett-Koehler books are printed on long-lasting acid-free paper. When it is available, we choose paper that has been manufactured by environmentally responsible processes. These may include using trees grown in sustainable forests, incorporating recycled paper, minimizing chlorine in bleaching, or recycling the energy produced at the paper mill.

Library of Congress Cataloging-in-Publication Data
Gelobter, Michel, author.
Lean startups for social change : the revolutionary path to big impact
/ Michel Gelobter ; foreword by Steve Blank ; introduction by Christie George.
        pages cm
Includes bibliographical references.
ISBN 978-1-62656-149-6 (pbk.)
1. Social entrepreneurship. 2. New business enterprises. 3. Business planning. I. Title.
HD60.G454 2015
658.1'1--dc23
            2015023961

First Edition
20 19 18 17 16 15   10 9 8 7 6 5 4 3 2 1

Project management, design, and composition by Steven Hiatt, Hiatt & Dragon, San Francisco
Copyeditor: Steven Hiatt   Proofreader: Tom Hassett   Cover designer: Irene Morris

To Nathan, Marco, and Troy

Maybe it is a better idea to let our lives teach us what to believe instead of making our lives conform to our beliefs.

Barbara Brown Taylor
Sermon, Riverside Church, July 14, 2013

Contents

Foreword

For over two decades, I worked in startups creating new products. When I retired and had to reflect on how new ventures were built, I realized that there was a more efficient way to use startup money, resources, and time. I developed a process called Customer Development and helped found a movement that embodied its core practices—The Lean Startup. This approach to innovation, along with business model design and agile development, are today transforming business as we have known it.

With this book, *Lean Startups for Social Change*, Michel Gelobter brings this powerful toolkit to the social sector.

The social sector has to keep up with, and in some cases outpace, changes in private markets to protect the noncommercial values and assets that form the bedrock of all we care about.

This book covers the core practices of the Lean Startup—how experimentation should supplant detailed planning, the critical practice of listening to customers (or "targets" in social-sector speak), and agility—while showing how nonprofit and government organizations can embrace these processes.

Innovation is vital to both the social sector and business, but the two do not operate, and therefore do not innovate, in the same way. Michel provides in-depth stories, examples, and tools to bridge these methods of innovation, relying on his years of experience in each of the relevant sectors—business, government, and nonprofit—to do so.

Michel and I met through our shared interest in the environment. He moved from social entrepreneurship to software entrepreneurship in the mid-2000s and contacted me to help with his first company. I went in the other direction. After I retired I started serving on nonprofit boards as chairman of Audubon California and then as a public official on the California Coastal Commission.

While I've helped accelerate innovation over the last three decades, I share with Michel a desire to repair the world we live in and to pass on to future generations a place with the same opportunities and beauty.

We must all learn to innovate, to change, to preserve what we most care about. With this book, Michel has made an invaluable contribution to that task.

Steve Blank
Pescadero, California

Introduction

What if we were building solutions that we knew worked rather than spending months or even years planning and simply hoping for the best? What kinds of problems could we solve? How many lives could we change? As the director of an investment fund focused on startups with social impact, I think about these kinds of questions all the time.

In 2011, the epilogue to Eric Ries's *The Lean Startup* suggested that an ultimate outcome of lean startup practice would be the creation of "new institutions with a long-term mission to build sustainable value and change the world for the better." The idea was to make new businesses that would build a better world.

Of course, the world is full of groups that already have that mission: nonprofits, government agencies, and organizations devoted to social change. Five years after the publication of *The Lean Startup*, I'm excited to introduce a book devoted entirely to them. Since *The Lean Startup* was first published, a thriving ecosystem of organizations and investors has emerged that's committed to learning how to make the social sector more effective through lean startup principles.

What is refreshing about social innovation is the scope and importance of the challenges being tackled. We're not simply optimizing to sell more widgets. Rather, social sector entrepreneurs are applying their creative energy and rigorous analysis to some of the world's most entrenched problems—problems that have persisted precisely because they resist easy solutions. This also means that we're solving problems that are too important to be left to the inertia of "what we've always done" and too vital to be addressed only with good intentions.

This is precisely what encourages me about this moment and about Michel's book. What the lean startup offers the social sector is a rigorous methodology to test new ways of solving problems. It provides organizations with a framework to quickly test new ideas and validate those that might be most effective. Critically, it saves social innovators our most valuable resource: time. Applying the lean startup methodology to social change allows for fresh experimentation that could transform society in ways that traditional social and business institutions may have overlooked or been afraid to try in the past. Lean startup thinking encourages us to get out of our heads and to test our proposed solutions in the real world to actually create massive, transformative social change.

When *The Lean Startup* was first published in 2011 the applicability of lean principles to the social sector was not yet as apparent as it is now. Early meetups were sparsely attended, and people expressed doubts that a business methodology could be applied to the social sector.

Fast-forward a couple of years, and we've seen everything from dedicated convenings on Lean Impact to a track for social innovators at the main Lean Startup conference. Most important, I've seen powerful examples of social change organizations applying lean principles to critical, world-changing work. Within our own portfolio at New Media Ventures, online organizing groups like SumofUs, activists for corporate accountability, are relentlessly focused on experimentation, routinely testing dozens of campaigns with their members before deciding—through evidence—which to focus on. Upworthy, one of New Media Ventures' early for-profit mission coinvestments, itself started as an experiment and has since been hailed as one of the fastest-growing media startups of all time. Upworthy's curators famously come up with twenty-five headlines for each piece of content they propose, alternatives that they can then test precisely to find out which headlines hook an audience.

We simply need more. We need more change and more progress, and we need more social sector organizations being effective agents of change. Finally, we need more specific examples of lean startup in practice in the social sector. This is where Michel's book comes in, and it provides a great start focused exclusively on nonprofit organizations and government agencies.

The task now is to scale the practice of lean startup in the social sector, but how do we go about doing that? It's not enough to highlight the work of social entrepreneurs. Funders play a critical role in advancing the cause. Some are eager to understand how to integrate lean's focus on serving real needs in a measurable way. Others are risk averse by design. Funders in government and private philanthropy are stewards of limited resources, and it can feel safer to support things that have *proved* effective rather than innovations that might simply "fail fast."

But I would suggest that the biggest risk funders face is not having *enough* impact. We're going to need to change the way we fund social sector organizations if we're to maximize our impact as funders. Because of its laser focus on measurement and experimentation (and, as Michel points out, service to those most in need of it), lean startup can actually provide the "validated learning" funders need to make better decisions every day about how best to spend their resources. Lean startup offers a way to elicit evidence of demand for specific solutions before a lot of money is spent.

Applying lean startup principles to the social sector or to the funding of social change is not without its challenges. Transformative social change can take a long time. Quick fixes and easy solutions are rarely available. Seemingly successful short-term solutions may have adverse long-term consequences, and when social change experiments fail, we fail real people in need. We all need to start sharing examples of what lean learning looks like in practice and destigmatize taking near-term risks to keep the focus on long-term benefits. I hope this book catalyzes honest conversations around these challenges and spurs us as a community to find creative solutions to address them.

Overall, a thriving culture of lean within the impact entrepreneur and funder communities could accelerate social change by removing taboos around experimentation and failure. If we can truly embrace the value of learning what works, then the social sector may be happily surprised by completely new innovative solutions that become widely adopted much more quickly than the forced models of the past.

Great nonprofits and great government agencies are not like great businesses. They are, first and foremost, effective agents of social change and uplift of the kind we all hope to be part of. With this book and with the growing lean startup community, we may be getting closer to that better world after all.

Christie George
San Francisco

1

Making Change the 21st-Century Way

Making change is hard—even before you start making it.

Whether you're in a big government agency, you're confronting a problem in your own community, or you're just trying to make a difference in a few people's lives, getting started is a challenge. You convene meetings, make plans, find partners, agonize over the right approach, cajole donors or funding agencies, compromise. You build a model that a lot of people sign on to, you secure funding, and you get started.

The stakes are especially high for making change in the social sector because failure is often not an option. In contrast with the private sector, social innovation requires something harder to get than money—it takes political and social will. If an innovation fails to deliver a vital product or service the momentum required to try again is often dissipated for years.

Aware of these stakes, the team you've assembled is working from a playbook you've painstakingly built, but you launch into a world that hasn't seen anything like this before. A new community forms around the idea. There's an excitement about the change that will come, an anticipation of the start, dreams about the middle and the end, about the time when the world, in some measure, will be a better place. Whether it's a new childcare center, an advocacy campaign to shut down a polluter, a trade association for dog trainers, or literally a new way of getting trains to run on time, a lot of work goes into gathering the energy and good will to get started.

And starting is when the real trouble begins. Sometimes the change you hoped to make actually happens, but, more often than not, there's a hard road ahead for your initial vision to actually manifest or for the change you hoped for to be big enough to make a difference. You work with the risk that all the planning and good will has been for naught.

To the founding team this process feels unique, but it is in fact the pattern of much innovation in business, government, and the social sector. It takes a tremendous amount of personal, social, and financial capital to get an idea off the ground, but all too often when the initial plan meets the real world the results are nothing like those anticipated.

Just over a decade ago, a revolutionary way to make change emerged from Silicon Valley: the lean startup. Companies were starting and failing so quickly that the startup pattern no longer felt unique. The lean startup alternative bypassed the freight of a plan and securing social and political capital behind it to focus on where the change actually has to happen and where the best-laid plans almost always run into trouble: in their direct encounter with customers.

The Lean Startup for Social Change

The lean startup turns the traditional, process-heavy approach to innovation on its head. It replaces detailed planning, consensus-building, and fundraising for something you aren't quite sure will work with speed, experimentation, and direct interaction with the people you are trying to reach. Initially the purview of software startups, the lean startup has jumped the fence to some of the world's largest companies, including Facebook, Google, and General Electric. Lean startup techniques are how these companies now regularly serve billions of people.

Social change advocates as well as a wide variety of traditional nonprofits and government agencies have also started adopting some lean startup techniques. The Obama administration launched the General Services Administration's 18F and then the broader US Digital Service to upend how the federal government delivers services. Mott Hall Bridges middle school in New York City's Brownsville neighborhood endowed a program fully in less than a week (and ultimately raised more money than it needed) to overcome the systemic bias that keeps qualified low-income kids out of the best colleges. Invisible Children, a faith-based student organization, reached tens of millions of people in one week to raise awareness of war crimes in Africa. By using the lean startup model for social change, these efforts delivered social innovation more quickly and with a higher return for all the blood, sweat, and tears that went into getting them off the ground.

Lean startup practice has just begun to take hold in the business world, but its implementation in the social sector is still rare and piecemeal. This book aims to change that so that innovators and leaders across the social sector can accelerate and expand their impact to meet the challenges of our times.

Change in Change Itself

The lean startup is radically more efficient than the old approach of driving human and financial resources into an elaborate but unproven plan. While it does not guarantee success, it accelerates the process of generating new understanding. For the business world, the lean startup holds the promise of being more revolutionary for the world than the emergence of industrial innovation in the 19th century. Where Frederick Taylor, Henry Ford, and others revolutionized *production* through rigorous study of industrial and human processes, the lean startup brings a radical new science to meeting the *demand* for products and services itself. In other words, the lean startup is designed, from the bottom up, to find the quickest, most efficient way of meeting a need.

What makes the lean startup possible are two fundamentally new capabilities that have emerged over the last two decades. First, it is possible faster than ever before to know the impact of a change you are seeking to make. Whether it's a change in people's behavior, their attitudes, or where they go day to day, or a change in the physical world, the instantaneous and ubiquitous connections that technology has enabled make it increasingly simple to know if that change is happening, and how. There is no single other factor that underlies lean startups more than this ability.

A secondary new factor is our ability to make small batches of almost anything faster than ever before. On the Web, in virtual space, we can test messages and product or service ideas in a matter of minutes by throwing up a webpage or buying click-words that magically appear in the lives of our target audiences. In the physical world, cheap, sophisticated product prototyping has been available for more than a decade in local markets or, with quick shipping, in emerging industrial nations like China and India.

This ability to quickly float a concept or a few samples of a physical product, when coupled with the ability to gauge its impact on people or the environment, almost instantly changes a whole lot about how we can conceptualize new products, services, and relationships and how we can scale them for maximum impact.

New products, services, relationships, scaled for maximum impact: the business sector is not alone in wanting these things. They are the lifeblood of progress in the social sector as well.

My Journey to Where Lean Meets Social Change

When I started my first company (a social venture called Cooler), I knew I wanted to make consumers a force for progress on global warming. I had already worked for almost twenty years as an environmental justice advocate, as a researcher, and as a government official, and with the passage of a number of groundbreaking laws on climate pollution, I thought I'd pushed the envelope on policy change as far as it could go in the mid 2000s. I wanted to keep moving people in the right direction, and I figured that I'd try to learn to go after them through their pocketbooks rather than the voting booth.

Cooler did OK as far as startups go. We were fast out of the blocks with terrific early customers, but slowed way down with the financial crisis of 2008. I realized that I had to start asking deeper questions about how to be effective in tough times.

My life changed the day I met Steve Blank. He'd been recommended to me as a "startup guru" and, luckily, we had a shared background as environmentalists. He met me at Kepler's, the famous Menlo Park café/bookstore of startup lore. Steve and I spent a few minutes looking at the impressive platform Cooler had built to tell consumers everything they wanted to know about how their personal spending was impacting climate change. We had a gorgeous interface that magically sucked data from people's bank accounts and calculated their global warming impact. Even better, we offered a menu of actions they could take to make the world a better place.

Steve cooed at all the appropriate places and I was feeling pretty good. Then he asked me to close my computer. He said that otherwise he'd be distracted by all the fun features. Then he turned to me and asked: "What's the one thing you most want people to do?"

We chatted and came up with a few good candidates for that one, top-priority, thing. After a bit of this discussion, Steve leaned in to me and, it felt, almost whispered: "You want to build something that *barely* works, but, if you took it away from people, they'd beg to pay you for it." I was in business then, and remained so for another eight years, but I knew I'd heard an insight for the ages.

I picked up Steve's book, *Four Steps to the Epiphany*, which, along with Geoffrey Moore's *Crossing the Chasm*, had already quietly become the bible for startups in Silicon Valley. I applied pieces of it to the clean-tech software companies I was starting or that I worked for. But I still spent a lot of my life on social change, advising friends in government and nonprofits about how technology could accelerate their impact, working at the board of directors level on strategy for the sustainability movement.

Thanks to Eric Ries's book *The Lean Startup*, the concept was growing in popularity as a transformative methodology for making new things in the business sector. And the social sector had a *lot* less money to deal with all the problems that were, by definition, too thorny for the private sector to take on. Surely these techniques were sorely needed to drive social as much as business change.

I started to see how the revolution that Steve's work was driving in business had equally powerful implications for those of us trying to drive social and policy change. Even more than in business, innovation in social change could be accelerated by the rapid feedback and rapid prototyping that was changing the for-profit landscape. The social sector's need for efficient ways to test and deploy new ideas was pressing.

Lean techniques also held the promise of dealing with some of the biggest frustrations of social sector innovation. So many social sector innovations are measured by how well they stick to "the plan" rather than by the impacts they have. In climate activism, for example, the real world news was always so hard to take: CO_2 emissions were steadily increasing, no matter what policies or campaigns we ran. So we measure our progress by membership or polling data or, even more remotely, by how many high-level elected officials and corporate leaders say that they believe in global warming. Because lean practice is based on new ways of measuring impact, it holds the promise of shifting the social sector to more useful, more immediate real-world measures as well.

At the end of the day, social change is about impact, and I started seeing advice, articles, and tools from the budding lean startup movement materially improve the work of my colleagues in the social sector and grow their impact. Startup nonprofits like Color of Change and the Citizens' Engagement Laboratory were expanding in scale and impact at unheard-of speeds.

Beyond impact, there are some critical additional reasons for the social sector to understand and to adopt lean practices. So many of the issues addressed by government and nonprofits are a result of business activities, and, thanks to lean startup processes, a whole bunch of new businesses are booming. From Facebook to Tesla to a host of "enterprise" software companies changing the basic infrastructure of government itself, the speedy transformation of our information and technology infrastructure has critical implications for justice and well-being across the board. The social sector needs to raise its game to keep up so that we can be sure that our values still guide the change rather than the other way around.

A Growing Movement

The good news is that it's already happening! The social and political stories of change highlighted at the beginning of this chapter illustrate how lean startup techniques are already driving unprecedented change in the social sector as well. As we'll see later in this book, each of the examples at the beginning of this chapter used one or more dimensions of the lean startup toolkit to achieve extraordinary results.

Furthermore, there are lean startup techniques that the social sector has been using since long before the lean startup movement began. (Listening closely to "customers"… well, that's called "organizing" in the labor movement.) What's important, though, is how these techniques form a coherent, whole approach to starting and growing an innovation. From end to end, lean techniques help at every stage of generating and developing a new idea.

The tools of lean startups are for a wide array of actors in the social sector, from the individual entrepreneur to managers in well-established nonprofit and government agencies. They are for employees seeking to excel, and for funders looking for transformative change. The lean philosophy is for elected officials who strive to make a deep and long-lasting impact.

But there's something else about the first examples in this chapter—about stories like Mott Hall School's mentoring program—that remains astonishing. They feel, in the parlance of Internet startups, like sightings of a unicorn, a rare, mythical creature. But what they have in common with stories about Google or Facebook or Amazon is the revolutionary role played by information technology. Like those companies, each of these social and political efforts used information technology to make change happen faster than it ever had before in their respective domains.

That's lean startups for social change—using lean techniques to achieve social and policy impact faster and more efficiently than ever before. And that's what this book is all about.

The lean startup has been on the cover of the *Harvard Business Review*, but it's still in its infancy, barely known outside Silicon Valley and a handful of business schools. It has barely begun to be adapted to nonprofit and government practice. This book introduces that practice: bringing the lean startup revolution into the field of social and policy change.

2

Lean Principles and Process

"Top of the heap ... in homelessness!"

That's what Monica Martinez said to herself after taking the job as CEO of Santa Cruz's Homelessness Services Center (HSC). Santa Cruz County, her new home turf, held the distinction of having the highest homelessness rate in America. Twenty-five years into the center's existence, Monica was determined to do something different. She was going to go lean.

For the past twenty-five years, HSC had followed the classic game plan: get an idea, write a plan, raise money (through charitable or governmental sources), and then carry out your plan. If you succeed at getting this far, then you take up what's next: measure impacts, evaluate, raise more money (see Figure 2.1).

This Plan–Fund–Do approach had served HSC well over the previous two decades. The organization had grown from a scrappy, community-led effort to a well-established provider of up to 145 beds a night for homeless people, with an annual budget of almost $2 million. All that planning and funding and doing had brought immediate relief to some of those suffering on the streets (18 percent of them on any given night), but it had done nothing to solve the problem permanently.

Monica was struck by the similarities with efforts to innovate in the private sector, where over 75 percent of startups eventually failed. In the nonprofit sector, the metrics were more multidimensional than simply whether or not you turned a profit for owners and investors. But the bottom line was the same in many ways. Any startup, any new program eventually had to answer the question: "Does it work?"

By that measure, HSC's efforts to end homelessness clearly had not. And there were twenty-five years of evidence to prove it.

The New Way: Lean Startups for Social Change

Information technology is the key factor profoundly transforming the way companies, nonprofits, and government agencies can drive change by closing the time (and sometimes the funding) lag between planning and doing. Cell phones, GPS, the Web, social networks, and many other transformative technologies allow social and business entrepreneurs to know *almost instantly* whether or not their actions, the steps they are taking to change the world, are working. This speed allows social entrepreneurs to bypass Plan–Fund–Do, instead disaggregating the process of innovation into smaller, quicker steps that can eventually grow far larger than ever before.

As steeped as we are in the Internet and cell phones, it's easy to forget all the ways in which our ability to get information has become faster and easier. For Monica's work alone, that means that many homeless people now have cell phones, or that her organization is notified by email whenever the county issues a voucher for housing.

Overall, this change in speed underlies the practice of the lean startup. For social change work, lean startup practice is guided by three core principles and by a process called customer development.

Figure 2.1 Plan-Fund-Do … Repeat

Principle 1: Fail Fast! (or, Everything Is a Hypothesis)

Instead of waiting for the plan … to get funded … then implemented, social entrepreneurs practicing lean start with educated guesses (or hypotheses) about how they expect the overall innovation to work. Then they test those guesses relentlessly, failing fast, but also speeding the way to development of solutions that actually do work.

Each element of how you intend to operate successfully is quickly mapped out, often on a tool called the Business Model Canvas. You lay out your core "guesses," but you test only those critical to early validation of your initiative. The model is broken down into vital components that can be tested quickly when the time is right. You develop hypotheses on the key components of your innovation, including your value proposition, who you're targeting, how much it will cost, and how much it can raise (covered in much more depth in chapter 4).

Prototyping

The focus is not on planning, but on relentless testing.

In Monica's case, she and HSC simply started trying new ways to put homeless people into permanent homes. Their early hypotheses centered on the importance of community involvement, developing good will on the part of landlords toward the homeless, and new partnerships (such as one between the local Veterans Administration and the county housing agency).

The HSC team had set a goal of housing 180 people at the highest risk of dying on the streets within thirty months. After twelve months, they evaluated their hypotheses and weren't happy with what they found. They had, in fact, housed 20 people, but their metrics showed that they would land far short of their goal and end up housing a total of 50 or fewer after thirty months of effort.

The lean startup methodology had emboldened Monica and her team to innovate, to measure, and to test. It also enabled them to learn. A year into the program they focused down to one hard number. In the language of lean startups, it was "the one metric that counts": the length of time between when a homeless person gets a housing voucher and when he or she signs a lease. *Problem and Solution*

They had failed fast. Rather than taking twenty-five years to understand the persistence of homelessness in Santa Cruz, the Homelessness Services Center had learned in just twelve months that their approach wasn't fast enough, even though it was still doing some good. They had not let themselves drift into change that was important but, finally, insufficient. Rather, they had experimented, measured, and found themselves wanting. Then they pivoted.

In the process, the lean approach had forced them to constantly revisit the most basic question: What are we trying to do? The single metric they settled on not only drove unprecedented results, but fully embodied their innovation and their intention—getting the homeless into homes.

Fail fast means getting out of planning mode and into testing mode, eventually for every critical component of your model of change. Customer development is the process that embodies this principle and helps you determine which hypotheses to start with and which are the most critical for your new idea.

The Process: Customer Development

Customer development is all about testing the right hypotheses at the right time with the right data.

When Thomas Bukowski thought of a way to help really sick people in low-income countries, one of the first things he did was get out in the field. He flew from San Francisco to Nepal to see firsthand how patients enter the system he was hoping to improve. Watsi, his nonprofit, crowdsources funding to help critically ill individuals get the treatment they need. Thomas wanted to go lean. It was out in the clinics of rural Nepal that he began to understand what that really meant.

One of the shorthand ways lean entrepreneurs refer to customer development is "get out of the building" because the key to its implementation is that the data comes from real people (your targets, your funders, your partners) in the real world, well outside the conference room where you came up with your hypotheses.

How Do You Feel about the Word "Customer"?

The word "customer" doesn't always fit the way the social sector works, but the toolkit already out there for customer development is so vast and applicable to the social sector that it's worth a little jargon to make sure that lean startup practitioners in the social sector have access to the most complete array of tools. Chapter 3 covers this distinction in some detail.

Besides relentlessly driving you toward feedback from outside your organization, customer development lays out a process that stretches from the very first hypotheses about what you are creating to the questions of how to scale your innovation and, eventually, how to institutionalize it for long-term sustainability and growth. It's a four-step process that helps you develop hypotheses appropriate to your stage of development and drives you to use real-world data (from customers!) to test them.

The discipline of customer development is the core framework for lean startups. We'll be devoting several chapters to each of its four stages. From end to end, they are:

Discovery. The initial stage of customer development involves translating your initial ideas about the innovation into hypotheses, testing assumptions about the needs being filled and the behaviors of key "customers" with respect to those needs. The key output of this phase is the simplest possible implementation of the program, called the minimum viable product (MVP), that allows for in-depth hypothesis testing. The focus is directly on the service or program to discover whether it can achieve its goals in as small an experiment as possible.

For Watsi, the MVP was simple. It test whether money to pay for critical healthcare could be channeled effectively to deliver that treatment. Watsi's founders didn't build software to do this. They worked with partners to identify the needy and sent money directly collected from their families and friends. At minimal expense they rapidly proved that individuals from across the world could directly save a life dependent on an expensive medical procedure.

Validation. The second stage broadens the range of hypotheses tested to include the broader environment, what it takes to get the program noticed, placed in use, paid for. This is often the point of first failure, where some key hypotheses start to fail. In almost every case, lean startups learn so much in this phase that they perform what's called a pivot. They learn lessons, redesign their approach, and turn to a new way of doing things.

The moment when Monica Martinez and the Homelessness Services Center realized that they weren't going to make their numbers was a pivot moment. They revamped their MVP to focus less on building a network and more on driving down time lags in the system.

Creation. With a proven, simple product in hand and a granular understanding of how targets, partners, and funders react to the new program, you focus in the creation phase on what it takes to grow rapidly. You test a new set of hypotheses around the problems of scaling and replication. How will you reach the average program customer? What medium (online, word-of-mouth, direct mail ...) will you use? Who will be the most effective messengers? What will be the range of reactions to different ways of reaching customers? In short, beyond the service or product itself, how can it be effectively delivered to the largest number of people at the least cost?

Watsi hasn't fully answered this question yet, and the answer will undoubtedly be complex. Beyond delivering money for healthcare, Watsi must understand the best ways to attract donors to its crowdsourcing platform. What will its long-term relationship be with the philanthropic community that supports its infrastructure? Are individual donors willing to see some portion of their contributions go toward organizational overhead?

Institutionalization. The final phase of customer development is institutionalization—shifting from the exploratory mode that launches and scales innovation to an operational mode that embodies all the lessons learned. Many hypotheses remain to be tested, but they tend to focus more on internal processes and how to keep improving and scaling impact in a more institutional way.

Lean startup practices are relatively new in the social sector, and not many of its practitioners' organizations have reached this phase yet. But as they mature, these organizations can draw on their counterparts in the private sector for inspiration, and we'll lay out some real-world cases in chapter 12. In a true lean organization, this phase can require the most creativity to keep the organization focused on ongoing innovation and prevent it from slipping back into expensive, inefficient ways of doing business.

Despite all this structure, customer development fosters tremendous creativity. The key is that it allows you to postulate the wildest possible hypotheses and then gives you a rigorous structure in which to test them efficiently and effectively. It helps social change entrepreneurs focus on the right questions at the right time, while taking nothing away from their tremendous creativity. On the contrary, it gives them a structured way to aim high and move quickly.

The second principle of lean startups for social change is all about *how* to test their hypotheses ... how to build your program and succeed in the fastest, cheapest way possible.

Principle 2: Agile Development

Worldreader started with a simple goal—to fill the empty shelves of schoolrooms across Ghana with books. Until very recently, literacy programs to achieve such a goal ran like classic, hierarchical bureaucracies, with long-term plans determined in distant capitals, flowing out into the field to splash up against the messy reality of communities where illiteracy is widespread. Without even realizing it, Worldreader turned centuries of Plan-Fund-Do literacy projects on their heads. David Risher, Worldreader's founder, said, "We were agile without even knowing it."

Principle 1 replaces the elaborate assumptions implicit in the old Plan–Fund–Do model with educated guesses to be tested quickly. Agile development (Principle 2) replaces the Plan–Fund–Do method itself with a new way of building things. Agile production methods offer fast, iterative ways of building change. At more advanced levels, they offer a blueprint for how to generate guesses about your project that have the best chance of being right.

Worldreader's experience started with direct experience with the problems of illiteracy and the absence of books in Ghana's classrooms. The few books that were there were wildly out of date and out of context (*A History of Utah* was a title on one school's bookshelf). You couldn't make this stuff up, but it was probably the residue of some elaborate previous plan to help educate Ghanaians.

One of the ways agile development works is by creating a story about users, often called *use cases*. From there, you work backward to scenarios and archetypes—fleshed-out ideas about the place of your innovation in its broader context as well as multidimensional portraits of the people you are trying to reach or serve. In Risher's case, he returned from Ghana with a clear vision of an entire generation leapfrogging paper books with digital ones, of getting the right tools and the right content to build literacy across the globe.

What he did next was the opposite of Plan–Fund–Do. He did not write up a long, detailed plan, and he did not seek funding. Instead, he asked Amazon for some Kindle tablets and smuggled them into Ghana preloaded with kid-friendly books like *Curious George*. The kids took to the books immediately and started looking for more culturally specific books, seeking new downloads.

Agile development is an ingredient to lean startups but a diverse field of practice in its own right with many streams and approaches useful to the social sector. What those diverse approaches have in common is that they can all be boiled down to one simple cycle: *Build–Measure–Learn.* Those three words capture the iterative nature of agile development. They are the way we make the product or service we are offering and how we test our hypotheses about the best ways to make it effective.

Agile development is the methodology that complements the customer-centered data gathering in customer development. As the name implies, agile development is also very much about speed. It is the method that can allow lean startup practitioners in the social sector to find the path to success quickly. Alternately, it's the method that helps you figure out why you're failing quickly enough to do something about it, or to revamp your approach as soon as possible.

The main imperative of agile development is to implement your innovation in ways that allow the fastest looping through the Build–Measure–Learn cycle. Contrast Risher's approach to that used by the famed One-Laptop-per-Child (OLPC) project. OLPC was an idea, born at the MIT Media Lab, to mass produce a great laptop for low-income children around the world. While its main goal was similar (basic literacy), OLPC took more than six years of design and building before producing a viable machine. But by then it had become clear that cell phones were already well on their way to penetrating the same markets with essentially the same capabilities as a simple, basic, relatively indestructible laptop. Almost fifteen years since OLPC was first conceived, they've reached over 2 million children. Those are great results, but Risher and Worldreader surpassed that number in two years.

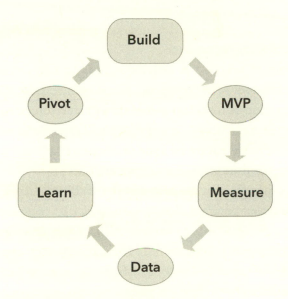

Figure 2.2 The Agile Way: Build–Measure–Learn

How fast is fast? To give you a sense of what "fast" in the agile world can mean, there are companies in the software business that release *dozens* of versions of their product every day. They take a little extra time up front and build diagnostics into the product itself so they can measure what each change has achieved in terms of product uptake, customer satisfaction, and delivery of essential functions right to the customer.

Most organizations, including nonprofits and government agencies, can't meet this standard right out of the box. But Build–Measure–Learn is not an abstract concept. Organizations can set goals for the iterative process itself. Worldreader's first few experiments took months: collecting Kindle tablets, smuggling them into different countries, experimenting with different content and ebooks. By steadily focusing on the rate of iteration itself, Worldreader can now prototype and test entry into a new community or serving a new type of user on a weekly basis.

As important as Build–Measure–Learn are the outputs at each step in that iterative process:

- The output of *build* is a minimum viable product (or MVP) based on feedback from customer development. It's the smallest, leanest possible implementation of the original innovation that allows testing of the most basic guesses about how to make change happen.
- The output of *measure* is data, used to evaluate the experiment that you ran with the MVP.
- The output of *learn* is what lean practitioners call a *pivot*, a revision of the original MVP meant to retest the original hypothesis, to test a revised hypothesis, or, if the original hypothesis is spot on, to move the product or service to the next level in creating even more value.

In sum, agile development is the process by which you actually implement your innovation and iterate it until it's explosively effective, or you give up. Agile is the toolkit for the experimentation that is key to lean startup.

To many in the social sector, the idea of trying multiple different approaches is scary. Innovation often has to happen in environments like jails or hospitals where there is already plenty of risk without adding an explicit focus on risky experimentation. And how are we supposed to fund multiple experiments in environments where people have barely enough to scrape by today? That's where the third principle comes in.

Principle 3: Efficiency!

Lean = Efficient. Lean's origins are in companies where you have to make big change with very little money. Which means you have to do everything else we've covered in this chapter—test hypotheses, engage customers, develop iteratively—as efficiently as possible, or else you'll run out of money before you've discovered how to grow and sustain your innovation, and then you will go out of business.

But efficiency is even *more* important to lean startups in the social sector because there's often more at stake when a social innovation fails than when a business one does. In 1991, I was director of environmental quality for the City of New York. The agency's budget regularly exceeded $2 billion per year, and that same year the agency was fined $750,000 (less than 0.05 percent of our total budget) by the state for the pollution we'd imposed on the Greenpoint/Williamsburg community through delay in cleaning up a major sewage treatment plant.

Fines against the city were usually left with the city to be spent on vanity projects that staff at agencies picked out. In a major departure from this practice, we convinced the state to force us to spend the money for the benefit of the same community we had polluted. In effect, we would empower the community with its own capacity to understand environmental conditions and independently verify the city's compliance with environmental laws and standards: we would conduct the first comprehensive, community-based, cross-pollutant environmental assessment in the United States.

We were pretty scared—because failure was not an option. At the end of the project, the community had to be better off, and the only other option on the table was to rebuild a billion-dollar sewage treatment plant from the ground up. Customer development hadn't crystallized as a widespread practice yet, but that's pretty much all we did. We met with community members, we made educated guesses about what they needed, we implemented them, and then we started that process all over again based on their feedback.

Despite the fact that we were one of the largest city agencies, we were aware from the beginning that we had to be super-efficient to pull this project off. The competing pressures of the project—diverse community demands, regulatory pressure from the state, budget constraints from City Hall, and the fact that several of the most egregious polluters were other state and city agencies as well as our own agency—meant that we had to show results despite limited time and money.

As nonprofit and government practitioners of lean startup iterate their way toward solutions, they face a number of pitfalls that a steady focus on efficiency can help them avoid. First, rather than being distracted by all the competing demands for innovation that arise in situations like the one I faced, the principle of efficiency forces teams to keep the discipline of building and testing to the smallest possible goal that will advance the innovation. Efficiency means making the leanest possible solution work, and the minimum viable product and customer development are tools for *efficiently* testing an innovation.

Second, as lean startup projects iterate and pivot based on what they are learning, they face budgetary and political/social constraints on how much they can really experiment. Keeping efficiency front and center kills these two critical birds with one stone.

Efficient spending on the smallest useful tests extends the financial runway for the innovation, giving change-makers more chances to innovate repeatedly on the limited budgets available for new initiatives in government and nonprofits. A focus on efficiency makes it easier to keep stakeholders like foundations, oversight committees, and the public in the loop on why you're making the choices you are.

Time is the enemy of all great innovations, and efficiency buys you the time needed to pivot until you've found the engine

I Innovation Accounting

of change you're looking for. In the private
world, small companies use a <u>tool called in</u>
that tracks how much each experiment costs
down the very cost of experimentation itself.
plies to governments and nonprofits as well is
limit to making your vision come true is the number of pivots
you have left.

One early finding in our work in Greenpoint was a potentially
elevated level of stomach cancer. A local Hasidic rabbi in fact simply ordered his congregation not to procreate for fear of bringing
children into its risk-laden environment. As I mentioned earlier,
running out of pivots in Greenpoint/Williamsburg was not an
option.

The Greenpoint/Williamsburg Environmental Benefits Project, as it would come to be called, eventually ==succeeded in addressing many community concerns== and, more important, giving
residents a sense of real control over their hazardous environment. It developed a comprehensive, community-based monitoring and assessment system that led to a number of further
innovations in urban sustainability across that community and
the country.

When you've got an impossibly big goal with impossibly small
resources, ==efficiency in design, in experimentation, in spending,==
==and in myriad other dimensions is absolutely essential to achieve==
==success.==

Summing Up

The lean startup is guided by three principles:

1. *Fail fast.* Move from Plan–Fund–Do to quick, educated
   guesses that generate data about your innovation's effectiveness.

2. *Agile development.* Quickly Build-Measure-Learn, and do it all over again until you find the optimal product or service, or until you fail, fast.

3. *Efficiency.* Preserve financial, social, and political capital by spending the least amount for the most result.

The overall process is customer development—a way of testing your guesses with the right people at the right time for each stage of growth in your program. By and large, these principles and process are interchangeable with those used by lean startup practitioners in the private sector, and this chapter has examined them in some depth. Before we plunge into the practices of lean startups, in the next chapter we'll take a look at key ways the social sector *differs* from the private sector, and the importance of those differences for lean practitioners in each.

3

The Difference a Sector Makes: Lean Startups for Profit versus for Social Change

I'll never forget the time that Vince, a chief financial officer I'd recently hired out of the private sector, walked into my office and asked, "So ... how do we make money?" He'd gotten on top of spending in record time and had a firm grasp of our burn rate—how much cash we were using each month to pay our bills. He'd reviewed payroll for any discrepancies or inequities. He'd established policies for promotions and new hires. The one thing he couldn't figure out was how we made money. And, strictly speaking, we didn't.

An organization's relationship to revenue is one example of a big difference between business and the social sector. There are others, including mission, hiring, relationships to those we serve, and the risk profile of the organization and its employees. Each of these is relevant to how the lean startup works for nonprofits and government.

The organization I was running at the time was the country's only sustainability policy institute (called Redefining Progress), and, in a good year, other organizations paid us $250,000 for our work. The rest of our $2.8 million revenue came from foundations and donors as charitable gifts. The fact that we didn't sell anything—that we couldn't project revenue from something whose production, marketing, distribution, and sales we could at least somewhat control—freaked Vince out. The dominant metric that Vince was used to driving was revenue, and we had a lot more on our agenda at Redefining Progress than that.

Making change is different from making money, and startups in the social sector have to worry about far more than revenue. The ability to generate large amounts of revenue has, appropriately, been the primary metric for lean startups in the business sector.

Lean practices can deliver incredible results for nonprofit and government innovators as well, but this chapter takes a little time to highlight the similarities and differences between the sectors so that lean startup practitioners can jump into that practice and benefit—without missing a beat—from the vast array of tools available.

The 3 Ms: Mission, Motivation, and Metrics

> In business, money is both an input (a resource of achieving greatness) and an output (a measure of greatness). In the social sectors, money is only an input, and not a measure of greatness.
> Jim Collins, *Good to Great*

Mission and Motivation

Katherine wakes up every morning with a fire in her belly. As she walks to her office in San Francisco, she gets tremendous satisfaction walking past the headquarters of corporations that have adopted her company's product. For several of them, she's actually calculated how many hours a year they save because they can now seamlessly share documents and other vital information, and that number is in the millions for enterprises in downtown San Francisco alone. She is a marketing manager at

Dropbox.com and is passionate about the speed with which its product is transforming how people work.

Joe feels the same way about his work as a transportation official in New York City. He bikes to work these days along streets that used to be forbidding to bicycle riders. He is a fiend for measurement—his agency has taken to just painting new bike lanes in place and letting the data on ridership determine whether they stay or go within a few months. He is still amazed at the feeling he gets in his gut when he stops at key intersections and sees crowds of new bike commuters thronging the street.

Katherine and Joe are both in the business of making change. They are motivated by a vision and values about what it means to make a contribution. Their choices about how to roll out their respective innovations are largely guided by what can make the biggest difference to those they are serving—customers in Katherine's case, and citizens in Joe's.

The only real difference in mission and motivation between the private and social sectors is the degree to which they can easily be boiled down to money. In business startups, there is a presumption that the value you are adding can easily translate into dollars and cents and that, eventually, your startup can collect that value in monetary form. Core to Katherine's marketing case is that those millions of hours of time saved by workers add up to tens of millions of dollars in savings and ultimately in value to shareholders. In most cases, her own motivation is measured in the amount of money she will personally gain from fulfilling her mission as well. In successful for-profit startups, alignment of motivations from top to bottom is a crucial ingredient to success.

Joe's new bike lanes also save money, but in far more diverse ways (less traffic, reduced gasoline use, reduced commute times, increased commuter health, and better air quality, among others), and those benefits accrue to a far more diverse set of stakeholders than employees and shareholders. The financial benefit in the social sector is, often by design, quite diffuse, with large pools of beneficiaries. Funders rarely expect a direct payback, but they are looking for benefits that accrue as broadly as possible. And Joe may be personally motivated by just one or two of the benefits of his work, like reducing air pollution or increasing exercise.

Katherine and Joe are both about creating change. In the social sector, impact remains the primary metric of success, while in business that impact must almost immediately translate into financial gain. This difference has several general implications (as well as some specific implications that we'll look at in the following chapters).

Metrics

First, nonprofits and government agencies practicing lean must define metrics appropriate to the innovation they are undertaking so that they can measure their experiments with rigor. In Joe's case, each new bike lane project had to show multiple, measurable benefits, including:

- Increased safety
- Reduced traffic congestion
- Increased bicycle usage
- Increased retail and commercial revenue in bike lane corridors

Multisided Markets

Technically, most social sector activity looks like what is called in business a multisided market—a market where the payers are not the recipients of the product or service. In such markets, startups have to test hypotheses about all the relevant market participants.

Second, social sector innovators must also focus on metrics that matter to their funders, metrics that may not be the same as the impact metrics. As a manager of a city agency, Joe had to weigh the risks of entrepreneurship for his budget. How many failed bike lanes could he afford to build before he lost the mayor's support, or before irked legislators cut his budget? More generally, which performance measures matter most to those funding the innovation? A shared understanding of the model of change between the funders and the innovators is always essential. In a lean startup, it's also vital that learning be shared as it evolves, so that all stakeholders understand why the strategy has changed as a result of previously defined metrics.

Third, social sector organizations often find it challenging to develop rigorous metrics. It can, for example, be difficult to measure activities aimed at educating the public or changing public opinion (absent elections). In the private sector, the bottom-line metric is a spending decision—you know your innovation is successful if your customer spent money on it sooner or later. Activities that don't directly sell to customers, like marketing, face the same challenge as many social sector activities, but at the end of the day they are benchmarked against sales. Similar bottom-line benchmarks exist for change-making (like the success or rejection of a ballot initiative as a metric of voter education), but those benchmarks are far more diverse. Agreement among funders, staff, and leadership to a strong culture of metrics is essential to the lean startup. That strong culture is, paradoxically, what can free you to innovate based on the results you see.

Before you feel too bad, remember that most business startups don't make money immediately (as a matter of fact, most fail). They, like nonprofits and government agencies, start by figuring out how to deliver real value. Then, and only then, do they turn to monetization.

Failure

We've already seen that failure is often not an option in the so cial sector. When for-profit innovations fail, the consequence is that opportunities for making money don't materialize. Had we failed in our work in Greenpoint/Williamsburg, the city would have had to find another way to assuage local fears about cancer, because those fears were real and residents had responded by applying a great deal of political and social pressure. When social innovations fail, the challenge isn't simply the failure of that particular effort, it's that the underlying social problems don't go away. The search for solutions must continue, and the social and political capital pressing for solutions must be deployed yet again.

The origins of an effort at social sector innovation are often tied up with this social and political capital. The "investors" are more diverse than simply funders and include local residents, politicians, and other types of sponsors. Practitioners of lean startup need to bring these stakeholders along for the journey by preparing them for the rigors of lean's Build-Measure-Learn cycle, and we'll explore some of the ways to do that in coming chapters.

There is also a bit of a paradox in lean startup between Principle 1 (Fail Fast!) and the fact that the status quo is unacceptable for many social problems. The lean startup offers a structured way through this paradox: problems that *must* be solved are often left to the social sector, but that does not preclude a problem-solving method that is not afraid of failure. Indeed, intractable problems are those that most need our most radical experiments on the route to success.

"Customers"

Much of this book lays out the customer development process that is core to the lean startup, adapting it from private sector startups for nonprofits and government agencies. In business, "customer" is well defined—it's the person who pays you. In the social sector, people served more often than not are *not* those who pay you, complicating the use of the term considerably.

For almost any nonprofit or government agency, the question "who's our customer?" is multidimensional. Take the case of Watsi. To make Watsi work, Thomas needed to test basic hypotheses about multiple constituencies. Because Watsi would often deal with life-and-death medical decisions, he had to test whether the basic innovation—providing funds for critical medical care—could deliver to specific individuals who were ill.

In his trip to Nepal, he learned how people came into the clinics Watsi was partnering with, how their treatments would be determined, and how he could gather stories to bring back to his second important constituency: donors who would fund the treatments. A third constituency, philanthropists supporting Watsi's operating expenses, needed to know about operations and management to feel comfortable investing.

Watsi's story illustrates the complexity of the word "customer" for nonprofits. One dimension shared with the for-profit world is that customers are people you serve, even if, in the nonprofit context, they don't actually pay you. For Watsi, these are the patients who receive critical healthcare. To some extent, it's also Watsi's partners, the medical clinics and providers who convert the money Watsi gives them into treatment for their patients.

There are at least two different types of people who do "pay" Watsi. The core operating model is to connect individual donors to patients in need, so those contributors are a critical "customer," as are the philanthropic donors who support the infrastructure that makes it all possible. Watsi directs 100 percent of individual donations toward medical care, so this other category of donors is actually the source of support for Watsi's operations.

The lean startup practice in our sector is relatively new, while customer development is an increasingly mature framework that is central to any modern lean approach, private, public, or charitable. Changing the terminology for the social sector at this point would cut the sector off from the rich toolkit and wisdom that have emerged over the last dozen years of private sector practice. So, in this book, we will continue to use the word "customer," particularly when discussing the details of the customer development process. We'll also use "target," "client," and "people served," depending on the context. The constituencies being served in the social sector break down into three general groups:

- *Direct targets*: people and organizations who are the primary recipients of the program or innovation. For Watsi, these are the critically ill patients who receive treatment.
- *Indirect targets*: people and organizations who are influenced via direct targets or other mechanisms, but who are not the primary recipients. In Watsi's case, there are a wide number of indirect targets ranging from, most immediately, the clinics Watsi supports by paying for medical treatment for individuals to, eventually, insurance and other health systems that can be transformed by increased revenue.
- *Funders*: the people and organizations that support the innovation or program.

For Watsi, there are in turn multiple types of funders:

- *Individual donors* who use Watsi to directly contribute to healthcare for the critically ill.
- *Watsi financial supporters* (individuals and philanthropic organizations) who enable Watsi to operate and to send 100 percent of individual donors' contributions to provide services in the field.

- *In-kind contributors* who donate services (legal, technical, software) and time. These include board members, law firms, and software companies.

Who you define as a customer and how will depend on your operating model. Table 3.1 provides more general examples of customer types in the social sector.

Raising and Making Money

Private sector or social sector, most innovations don't start with money. They start instead with passion, a big problem, and a good hunch, and then they apply a lot of elbow grease. But once the project has legs, a critical factor for any startup is how to bring in money to finance growth and achieve sustainability.

Growth capital for innovation can take many forms. In the for-profit sector, the typical model is investment by individuals or institutions, and here businesses have two advantages over the social sector. First, they can offer a return on investment secured by ownership of stock or company assets. Second, they can raise funds based on human and intellectual capital. For companies like Coca-Cola these so-called "intangibles"—their brands, their people, their recipes—can constitute as much as 80 percent of their value. Even marketing disasters, like the New Coke fiasco of 1985, can eventually raise the company's value. Lessons learned, for better or for worse, are a form of capital in the private sector.

By contrast, consider Redefining Progress, the think-tank I ran in the 2000s. We had a website garnering 4 to 6 million hits a day and a trademarked brand (the Ecological Footprint) spread on more than 120,000 websites, but we had no way to borrow or raise investment directly against those assets. It's much harder, if not impossible, to capitalize intellectual property and human resources in the social sector.

Table 3.1 Defining "Customer" for the Social Sector

Customers and Their Relationship to Program: The "Customer"...	Sample Organizations or Programs	Examples of "Customers"
Purchases program services	Membership organizations (NRA, Sierra Club, kids' sports leagues) that provide services to members based at least partly on dues	Dues-paying members
	Most schools and universities	Students
Changes because of the program	Political campaigns	Voters
	Organizing campaigns	Local residents
	Public health campaigns	Workers in a particular setting; individuals at-risk or carrying a particular disease
Adopts/adapts behavior because of program	Voter registration drives	Nonvoters who become voters
	Boycott campaigns	Consumers
Receives goods or services from the program	Food distribution programs	Homeless people
	Scholarship programs	Students
	Hospitals	Sick people
	Libraries	
Uses the program or its outputs	Recreation centers	Kids/adults who practice sports
	Federal Aviation Administration	Airlines
Supports the program	Foundations	Actual funders: these can be foundations, donors, or members
	Individual donors	
	Members	

Social sector organizations have far fewer ways to raise financial capital, so they must be even *more* efficient than for-profit organizations in using that capital, and lean techniques can be a major asset in doing so. But it's also important that social sector investors understand the value of failure in building that human and intellectual capital.

Funders of early-stage social innovation usually have no expectation of a return on their investment. The primary sources of such capital for nonprofit and government innovators are grants or gifts from individuals and/or charitable or government sources. The ability to raise significant funding that, like grants, incurs no obligation to pay it back could be seen as an advantage, except for the fact that the vast majority of social sector efforts will require external capital not just to grow but to operate for their duration.

Another issue is Vince's original question: "How do we make money?" Beyond the startup investment, many successful, mature social sector innovations simply do not make money in the long run and must rely on gifts and grants to a large extent for their ongoing operation. Beyond the "customers" they serve, innovative programs, as they mature, must treat their funders as a form of customer as well to ensure ongoing support. For government programs, those funders are often budget offices, legislators, and, ultimately, the public. For nonprofit organizations, the funders are individuals, members, foundations, and government agencies.

Because social sector outcomes are so diverse, their work across the board has often been plagued with inappropriate performance metrics. The most pervasive metric is probably that of overhead, or how much of a nonprofit or government agency's overall spending goes to administration versus delivering services. Rather than measuring the overall impact of products or services, nonprofit rating agencies (like GuideStar and Charity-Watch) have, until recently, evaluated how much of a program's budget is spent on fundraising, administrative, and management tasks.

The focus on overhead *is* appropriate in a startup's early stages. Spending needs to be focused first and foremost on finding the right product or service and demonstrating impact. But once a repeatable business model has been found, the relationship of overhead to overall spending is relatively unimportant compared to what it takes to run the model successfully—for maximum impact.

The importance of social sector funding models cannot be overstated in the lean startup process. A few points therefore stand out for lean startup practitioners:

- Funders of nonprofits and government agencies running on lean principles must explicitly recognize that each failure generates vital learning (intellectual capital). How does the funding build in a way to preserve and transmit that learning to the field? How does it preserve and grow the human capital generated in those failures as well?

- Lean startup practitioners need funders who understand that you will be measuring outcomes but also your impact on the funders themselves, since they too are a client in the social sector.

- Some forms of private sector innovation are hard to link to near-term revenue (network effects models—"if we build it they will come"—for example), and the same is true in the social sector. Social sector investors may be skittish about investing where the outcomes are too distant from the day-to-day activity. Think-tanks are a great example of this category, where hard outcome measurement is chal-

The Overhead Debate

In 2002, Dan Palotta and his company ran the most successful breast cancer walks in history, raising a net amount somewhere over $70 million for that year alone. The following year, after controversy over the overhead involved led to sponsors dropping him, the net take for breast cancer dropped by 84 percent to less than $14 million. This story and others like it are leading to a reexamination of criteria for evaluating how much overhead spending is too much.

lenging. The most generously funded think-tanks are often those linked to direct returns to their donors. For example, those devoted to lowering taxes on the wealthy have proven returns to the wealthy who contribute to them, and those devoted to influencing foreign policy deliver results to governments or private interests who fund them.

- Overhead measurement for its own sake is meaningless. Overhead is just another part of the operating model, and it is the impact level and overall success of that operating model that is the vital metric.
- Since funders are critical customers, open communication about the operating models being tested is critical, as well as how agnostic the funder is willing to be about how its money is being spent. A socially conservative funder may reasonably be unwilling to fund needle exchange programs even if they are proven more effective at stemming diseases than spiritual counseling.
- A focus on overhead *is* appropriate in the early stages. Staying lean and hiring only those employees you need is vital at this stage.

Risks: The Stomach for "No Pain, No Gain"?

Funder (or Investor) Risk

Risk and innovation go hand in hand. When you start a new company, the major risk you face is not succeeding. Some argue that a tolerance for failure is the defining characteristic of Silicon Valley—that it is the only place on the planet where the experience of failure is almost as valued as the experience of success.

The key difference for the social sector, though, is that more is at stake than simply not making money. When you innovate for social change, the major risk you face is what economists call "opportunity cost." Opportunity costs are the costs incurred by having tried something at all. Everybody has limited time and attention, and each time you choose to do something there is a risk that doing something else would have led to a greater return.

Nonprofit funders seem to feel that opportunity risk more than for-profit funders. When for-profit investors and entrepreneurs make a risky investment on a new initiative, it's a given that they may lose all their money, and also a given that the payoffs (or upside risk) are substantial. In the social sector, funders are less sanguine about the risks they are incurring because they are constantly trading off donations to one cause versus another. There's not as clear a metric at the end of the day as there is in the private sector (return on investment). Instead, there is some real regret that, but for that risky failure, more good could have been done.

Individual Risk

The upside risk to individuals is also a consideration. Founders of for-profit startups are at least partly motivated by a big financial upside, whereas social entrepreneurs are often considered to risk nothing but reputation. Consider, though, the longer-term risk profile. A business entrepreneur may take big risks a number of times in her career, counting on luck and experience to lead to one or two "home runs" financially speaking (big bonuses, stock options, and other advantages) that provide a basis for retirement and security as she ages. A social sector entrepreneur has no similar "home run" horizon, at least financially. It's not news that you don't make as much money in the social sector, but the emphasis in the lean startup on fearless exploration and failing fast brings home the individual dimensions of these career choices.

Risk to "Customers" or the Field

Remember the "fail fast/can't fail" paradox we discussed earlier? A corollary is that, because social and political capital is a key part of social sector innovations, there is a risk that the experimentation inherent in the lean startup will wear out not the financial capital, but the political and social will necessary to take action. The innovation may itself lead to participants in the relevant field getting "innovation fatigue." An extreme example of this may be public support for the US war in Iraq. Given bottomless political will, the US military might eventually have found a way to stabilize that country, but the public's appetite for continued involvement and Iraqis' own patience for foreign occupation clearly wore thin well before a stable political and military situation could be established.

Inertia or even backpedaling can overcome a social sector initiative that takes too long or makes too many pivots in its search for a solution. Opponents of the innovation (think insurgents in Iraq) may also capitalize on this fatigue. This is a risk that also needs to be carefully managed in any situation, but one a lean startup particularly needs to deal with.

There are more differences between the for-profit and non-profit sectors, but this chapter has covered those most important to making the lean startup happen. It's time to start making change!

4

Discovery I:
The Nine Guesses

Discovery is the beginning of the journey to make the change you want to see. It's where you hone your vision and start testing it against reality.

The big difference between lean startup and everything else you've ever done is that you start with hypotheses—educated guesses about what you are seeking to change informed by your innovative idea. In discovery you will detail and deepen your initial vision and, most important, test it against the real world. You will "discover" how real people understand the problem and respond to your solution.

There are four steps that immediately get you out in the world and testing your vision:

1. Write down your best guesses for the critical elements of your innovation.
2. Test the problem.
3. Test the solution.
4. Verify or pivot.

Let's get started with the guesses!

Write Down Your Best Guesses: The Lean Change Canvas

The first step in discovery is to get all the hypotheses you have about your innovation written down in one place. The Lean Change Canvas in Figure 4.1, adapted from Alex Osterwalder's book *Business Model Generation*, is a good tool for putting all your best guesses on one page. The nine boxes of the canvas represent the key elements of almost any kind of business or operating model. The outcome, a one-page summary of all the hypotheses to be tested, becomes a scorecard you'll use until your innovation is proven and scaled. It is also an explicit, nine-part model of how your innovation will run.

I'll cover each box in the canvas in some detail, but first here are some practical guidelines about how to use it:

1. *Do it fast.* Don't give the canvas too much thought initially. Simply sit down and write out your vision, filling out as many boxes as you can in a fifteen- to twenty-minute session. You can do this with a group or by yourself, but in the spirit of experimentation it's always more interesting to start with individual versions. Then, if you have partners or colleagues who generated their own versions, you can compare notes and learn up front how many of the newly recorded hypotheses are already shared by the team and what to do about those that aren't. (Hint: Test them!)

2. *Different boxes are more important at different times.* You don't need to have a great hypothesis for every box. You must start with a compelling value proposition and a problem or problems that need to be solved. From there you can fill in the boxes as appropriate given the stage of your effort and your data-gathering. A good guideline is that the hypotheses in the canvas will be tested from right to left, starting almost immediately with the hypotheses about the targets and gradually moving across the grid to

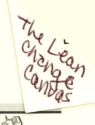

The Lean Change Canvas

Designed for: Lean Change

Designed by: Michel Gelobter

May 26, 2014

Iteration v1.1

Partners

Who are Key Partners or suppliers?
What activities do they perform?
Which resources do they provide?

Key Activities

What Key Activities do our Value Propositions require?
Our Channels?
Our Relationships?
Our Revenue streams?

Key Resources

What Key Resources do our Value Propositions require?
Our Channels?
Our Relationships?
Our Revenue streams?

Value Propositions

What *problems* are we helping to solve?
What value are we creating, for the world, for our funders, for our targets?
What is the *solution* (bundle of products and services) we are offering to each target?
What needs are we satisfying for whom?

Relationships

What type of relationship does each type of target and partner expect us to establish and maintain with them?
Which relationships do we already have, and what role do these relationships play in our theory of change?
How much do these relationships cost?

Channels/Pathways

What are the channels we will use to reach our targets?
How do we reach them now?
How many channels are there and how do they work together?
Which ones are most effective?
How are we integrating them with our targets' routines?

Targets

Who are the most important people we are serving or creating value for (include funders here)?
Who is providing us with revenue?
What types of people are we serving and interacting with?

Expense Structure

What are the most important costs inherent in our operating model?
Which Key Resources are most expensive?
Which Key Activities are most expensive?

Revenue Streams

How will this work be funded (sales/fee-for-service, donations, grants)?
How much will each funding stream contribute?
What will each potential funder be willing to pay for/contribute to?
What do prospective funders currently pay for/contribute to?
How are they currently paying/contributing?

Figure 4.1 Lean Change Canvas

things like which partners are essential and what the expense structure is likely to be.

3. *Put all your ideas on one canvas to start with.* You may have several ways to solve your chosen problem and/or several different types of targets requiring completely different channels. Start by putting them all in one place and then divide them up logically into separate canvases later. You can also use color coding to do this, coding each set of approaches with the same color.

4. *Keep it short.* The discipline of brevity forces your hypotheses to be clear and testable. If they are long and elaborate, use this as an opportunity to break them down into simpler sequences and start testing at the beginning. Watsi didn't start by testing whether people would give to help strangers with medical expenses. They started first with whether they could deliver *any* money at all to strangers, using their own money and waiting to test whether others would contribute until later.

5. *Work incrementally from the present.* Another way to keep your hypotheses direct and to the point is to start with the here and the now. Ask yourself, "What is the immediate next thing that must be true for this model to work?" For example, rather than hypothesizing "Foundation X will fund our initiative," try "Program officer Y will take a call to discuss our idea." Remember, the canvas is a living document. As each hypothesis is confirmed or rejected, note that learning on the canvas and add the next set of critical hypotheses.

  Finally, if you aren't coming into this exercise with a very clear idea of how to solve the problem you're trying to address, there are a number of approaches for generating operating models online at our website www.leanchange.net.

Filling Out the Lean Change Canvas

Initially fill each of the nine boxes in the canvas with one or more hypotheses. The Lean Change Canvas template in Figure 4.1 shows questions embedded in each box as prompts for generating the right hypotheses, and the answer to each of these questions is one or more hypotheses. The discovery stage focuses on making sure you understand the problem and that you've crafted a solution that could actually work for those you're targeting. So the most important boxes in the early stages of an innovation are Value Proposition and Targets, followed closely by Channels/Pathways and Revenue Streams.

To help you speed through this step, I've chosen four examples of diverse social sector projects to illustrate how to fill out the canvas for a diverse range of innovations. They are simplified case studies drawn from real-world nonprofit and government projects, not all of which were successful!

- *Smarter, Cleaner, Stronger.* SCS was the economic element of a legislative campaign for the Climate Stewardship Act between 2003 and 2007.
- *Catalog Choice.* CC is a behavioral/norms campaign to reduce junk mail.
- *The National Museum of the American Indian.* NMAI at the Smithsonian is an example of a major infrastructure project undertaken by a government agency.
- *The New York City Toilet Bowl Retrofit Program.* NYCTB was a ten-year, $300 million water conservation program that reduced water consumption in the city by 25 percent.

For each box, I'll sketch out key hypotheses for the different projects to help illustrate how to use the Lean Change Canvas in practice.

1. Value Proposition

This box is really about two dimensions of your value proposition—the problem you're solving and the solution (product or service) you're creating. They'll both be tested in steps 2 and 3 of discovery, respectively.

For the first dimension, enter problems your innovation will solve. Write some of the people you will solve it for into the Targets box. Follow your gut, name existing "solutions" as potentially part of the problem, and state them as plainly as you can.

The second dimension of your value proposition is the solution you are proposing. In business, the solution is often narrowly framed in terms of benefits to customers. In the social sector, there are often beneficiaries well beyond the specific people your innovation is targeting. For example, if you're targeting legislators for a change in a law, the question "What value are we creating?" needs to apply to them, but also to those who will benefit from the proposed changes.

It's OK not to be too sure about your solution at this phase too. The next step in the discovery process is to test your hypotheses about the problem with little regard at first for the solution. The interviews you conduct in the next phase may change your sense of the solution considerably. So stay flexible at this point!

As part of the Value Proposition box, you can put in specific statements about how your innovation will work, for example, "Users will log on to Catalog Choice." What service or product do you think will get you to the change you're trying to create? Finally, what needs are you filling? Needs are distinct from problems. For example, the problem being addressed by Smarter, Cleaner, Stronger was the lack of votes in the US Senate for climate change legislation. The need we filled by making an economic case for action on climate change was to give senators a nonenvironmental rationale for supporting the bill. By listing the need as a hypothesis like "Economic benefits to key states can shift their senators' votes," you can test in the following steps how important that need is to key constituencies, in this example US senators. You should also remain open to filling that need in a way that doesn't depend on solving the problem as you have already cast it. In the SCS example, if the economic rationale was inappropriate or ineffective, perhaps the support of another constituency important to senators like faith-based organizations or key minority groups could be brought to bear to secure their votes.

Another way to fill out the Value Proposition box is to write a brief story about how your innovation will help somebody. The story can explicitly name the problems as well as how your innovation will work. I provide an example of such a value proposition for Catalog Choice in Table 4.1.

By the way, it's never too early to think about how you're going to name or brand your innovation, and this is the time to start testing not just for the idea itself but also for what you're going to call your initiative. Kristen Grimm, in her great campaign planning manual *Just Enough Planning Guide*,[1] describes some of the messaging thinking behind Catalog Choice.

While the campaigners' goal was to reduce the waste of excess catalogs, consumers liked getting *some* catalogs and would react badly to a guilt-inducing environmental message. They settled on the name Catalog Choice as a way to convey the core value propositions of reducing mailbox clutter and giving consumers control over the catalogs they received, all the while doing better by the environment.

Chapter 7 of Kristen Grimm's guide is an excellent resource for considering how to name your initiative for maximum impact,

---

1 See her website, www.justenoughplanning.org/.

and Resources section of the website lists a number of services you can use to test your key messages quickly and inexpensively.

Table 4.1 provides examples of how to fill out the Value Proposition box for each of the four case studies.

2. Targets

This box is for your hypotheses about all the people your innovation will serve. As we discussed in chapter 3, the map of "customers" for social change is considerably more diverse than the traditional business definition of customer, but you can start with the generic categories discussed in chapter 3—direct targets, indirect targets, funders, or the more detailed set of archetypes laid out in Table 3.1.

Get specific here with a strong bias toward early adopters no matter what type of target you're talking about. Most true innovation is not going to appeal to the mainstream market right away, so for purposes of testing and validating your hypotheses, think specifically about those *most* likely to initially adopt or be influenced by what you're going to send out into the world. In addition to the target type, consider listing targets by the *roles* they're expected to play in the innovation. For Smarter, Cleaner, Stronger, newspaper editors were a major target for the research on the economic benefits of acting on climate change. The senators were indirect targets compared to the editors we tried to reach directly. The editors' role was to be influencers, people who shape the senators' daily political environment.

It's possible to really go to town in this box, and you should determine the level of detail you want to go into initially versus additions you can make further down the road. Some of the dimensions to consider as you hone in on your targets include:

Table 4.1 Sample Value Propositions

Smarter, Cleaner, Stronger	National Museum of the American Indian	Catalog Choice	New York City Toilet Bowl Retrofit
Problems	**Problems**	**Problems**	**Problems**
4 to 6 US Senate votes short of passing climate legislation	Native American artifacts poorly stored and inaccessible.	Unwanted catalogs waste tremendous amounts of paper	Hard for consumers to save water on their own
Influential people in home states unconcerned with action on climate	National collection housed in isolated New York facility	Consumers have no control over the catalogs and junk mail they get	Water conservation equipment is expensive and installation costs unpredictable
Solutions	New York unwilling to cede control over collection	**Solutions**	**Solutions**
Economic benefits to key states can shift their senators' votes	**Solutions**	Give consumers choice over catalogs they want	Subsidized, regulated toilet bowl retrofits
Economic actors in key states can be mobilized to pressure senators to change position	Move collection to new facilities	**User Story Alternate**	Give plumbers incentives to retrofit routinely
	Maintain significant presence in New York	Massive amounts of paper are wasted because of unwanted mail-order catalogs. Catalog Choice will allow consumers to:	
		• Reduce the junk mail cluttering their mailbox	
		• Control the catalogs they get	

- *Their relationship to the problem.* Are they aware of it (urgency)? Are they motivated to change it (active versus passive)? Are they already working on it?
- *Stories.* You can write up detailed stories of how key users will encounter your innovation as a way of generating additional hypotheses about how to move forward. For the National Museum example, the planners had to assess how researchers would be affected by the new museum, its location, and how it stored the overall collection.
- *Archetypes.* What are key characteristics of your targets that you should consider in designing your innovation? For the National Museum, how do researchers differ from simple museum patrons or corporate sponsors?

Your targets also don't operate in a vacuum, and your innovation should be designed with a sense of how they make decisions and whom they interact with along the way. Consider mapping the way they work and/or their key influencers. There are many tools for doing this, but an important one for the social sector is power mapping (see Moveon.org's great resource for this at leanchange.net/powermap). The power map includes actors who may not even be targets for your innovation, like those opposed to your campaign or service, but the exercise will help you think through the elements of your innovation that must account for opposition, and this will be invaluable in the next phase of customer discovery—validation.

Table 4.2 shows sample entries for the Targets box for each of our case studies.

Table 4.2 Sample Targets

Smarter, Cleaner, Stronger	National Museum of the American Indian	Catalog Choice	New York City Toilet Bowl Retrofit
Direct	**Direct**	**Direct**	**Direct**
Newspaper editors	Museum-going public	Consumers who get mail	Plumbers
Congressional staff	Researchers	**Indirect**	Plumbers Union
Local academics	Native communities looking for a repository for cultural artifacts	Catalog companies	**Indirect**
Local business-people		Mail-order retailers	Consumers
Indirect	**Indirect**	Environmental NGOs	Building owners/managers
Senators			**Funders**
Funders	**Funders**	**Funders**	City Office of Management and Budget
Foundations	Congress	Foundations	
Labor unions	Smithsonian trustees		
Clean energy companies	Tribes		
	Individual donors		

3. Channels/Pathways

Channels and pathways are how your innovation gets to your target. They represent the specific links between your organization and the people you hope to serve, influence, or change. The channel can be physical (NMAI is an actual facility that real people visit every day); written/spoken (Smarter, Cleaner, Stronger relied on written reports delivered to thought leaders); or virtual (Catalog Choice reached people online for their selections). The choice of which pathways or channels you will use to drive change is critical.

The first channel to list is the one closest at hand. As you launch your innovation, you will be speaking with lots of targets in the next two steps. The way you plan on reaching those folks (online, door-to-door, structured interviews, casual visits) is your first channel.

The converse is to make sure to think about the biggest channels you could use. You'll be speaking with lots of people as you get started in the next few weeks, and what you learn from them, their interest in adopting your innovation, will be exciting. But face-to-face interviews and interactions are just one channel to impact. Don't get so caught up in the immediate that you neglect the truly scalable channels that you might develop.

In 2002, my colleagues and I started something called the Climate Justice Corps to train young people to fight global warming based particularly in communities at the front line of impacts. We recruited from schools around the country and for the next few years trained ten to twelve young people per year. Our goal was to give communities of color a voice in the climate debate, and our channel was to work through our corps members directly with communities. By the program's third year, we realized that we had the potential to train thousands of young people by shifting to a multilevel marketing model. Unfortunately, we had come to this realization too late, and our training costs of upward of $10,000 per student for a summer eventually dragged the program down. Since then, other organizations, notably the Alliance for Climate Education, have adopted that model and reached over a million young people to date.

So make sure to put some really big ideas for channels on the Lean Change Canvas as well, because there's nothing worse than going down a successful pathway that, at the end of the day and with a lot of effort, just doesn't get to the scale needed by the challenge you are addressing.

Channels in the business sector can be diverse but are limited by the fact that they are all about collecting revenue from customers. Untethered from this requirement, social sector channels can be designed with great creativity. I won't attempt to create a typology here, but consider factors like:

- Are you charging for your service or product? Do you have to design the channel to collect revenue, to be self-funded, to use a sliding scale, to be subsidized, or to use some other pricing mechanism?
- Do your targets come to you, as on a blog or in a museum, or do you go to them, as in door-to-door organizing?
- Is your service "self-serve," through your website or online service, for example, or direct, as in when you deliver the product or service directly yourselves?
- Are referrals an important part of your channel strategy? Do you need your targets to be enthusiasts, evangelists?

Remember, you will likely start with direct contact with your targets. All these other channels will come later. Their success will be built on understanding exactly what works for the people you are trying to reach. That early hands-on emphasis is critical to testing your innovation and reaching a great outcome. Only when you understand the granular appeal of your innovation will you truly start exploring channels and pathways that allow for rapid growth in your impact. Table 4.3 shows sample entries for the Channels/Pathways box for each of our case studies.

4. Relationships

This box on the Lean Change Canvas focuses on the relationships you will have to your targets. This is not so much a mechanical listing of links to the targets so much as a set of hypotheses about the tangible and emotional relationship you will have with the people and organizations you are targeting. What type of relationships do you already have, and how will those change as a result of your innovation? How will your targets first become aware of you? What will the ongoing relationship be like, and how will your targets themselves help you spread your innovation? Finally, what will it cost to have these relationships and what kind of revenue might come in return?

Table 4.3 Sample Channels/Pathways

Smarter, Cleaner, Stronger	National Museum of the American Indian	Catalog Choice	New York City Toilet Bowl Retrofit
National environmental campaigners State-level environmental groups State and local business-people	New buildings in New York City and in Washington, D.C. Online/digital resources	Google AdWords Environmental partners News stories Large identity management firms such as Experia and Verisign	Plumbers Union Large independent contractors

The more human the relationships the better. We all know that a visit to a senator's office is better than sending a white paper. At the same time, the Relationships box offers one of the most concrete places to test hypotheses in numerical terms. One way to visualize this is the double-ended funnel used in the business world to embody three key relationship tasks:

- *Get*: How will you actually engage or "sell" your targets on your innovation? How will you lead them through the process of becoming aware of you, being interested, consider-

Figure 4.2 Get-Keep-Grow: The Relationships Funnel

ing the change, and then finally engaging with or buying into the innovation you've created?

- *Keep*: How will you keep the relationships you establish? How will you let your targets know you are paying attention and using their feedback or adapting to changing conditions they face?

- *Grow*: The best way to grow your innovation will likely be by building on the relationships you already have. Can you get new relationships by unbundling parts of your innovation or offering customized versions tuned to specific needs? Can you offer more of your service or product, or expand your relationships to additional pieces of your innovation from their original engagement? Your reputation with your targets and their willingness to testify to the value you are creating is probably the most important way to grow as a social sector innovation. Not only does their good will and positive experience help attract others in the field, it is a big predictor of foundation and donor interest as well.

There's a lot to be said about the role of relationships in social sector innovation, and it's very easy to get caught up in elaborate plans for all three elements of this funnel or whatever other long-term framework you adopt to develop your relationships. At this early stage, just put your thoughts on the canvas and get out and test. Then keep revisiting the questions raised as you develop your relationships. Table 4.4 shows sample entries for the Relationships box for each of our case studies.

Table 4.4 Sample Relationships

Smarter, Cleaner, Stronger	National Museum of the American Indian	Catalog Choice	New York City Toilet Bowl Retrofit
Get	***Museum visitors***	***Get***	***Plumbers***
Use of locally branded materials	Members	Websites, apps, banner ads, blogs, news stories	Retrofits become core business
Meeting with editorial boards	Occasional visitors		Retrofits generate additional work/revenue at all jobs
	Once-in-a-lifetime visitors	***Keep***	
Keep		Customization	***Building owners***
Steady stream of newsworthy research and stories	***Researchers***	Increase categories of junk mail served	"Pull" model where owners request retrofits to save money
	Physical repository		
Locally relevant research	Online repository	Online help	
	Native communities	***Grow***	
Grow		Referral rewards, contests, additional services	
Local websites	Expert advice on artifact preservation		
	Repository for key cultural artifacts		

5. Key Resources

What are you starting with? What do you need to succeed? Your guesses about these things fill the Key Resources box on the Lean Change Canvas. There are at least five types of resources to consider as you fill out this part of the canvas:

1. Intellectual property 2. Physical Assets 3. Financial Resources 4. Good Will 5. Human Resources

Intellectual property. IP is traditionally underused in the social sector because, compared to businesses, nonprofits and governments can't convert IP into money. (Businesses often formally value their IP in loan applications or stock offerings, for example.) A rigorous approach to managing the new ideas you're creating can still add incredible value to your innovation. Trademarks are among the easiest form of IP to manage because, by law, the mark is established as soon as you start using it (and using a little ™ logo along with it).

The key is to be consistent in your use and, if you decide that trademarked IP (like logos and slogans) are critical to your success, to defend your trademark by challenging others who misuse it so that it doesn't degrade. An example of an important but legally degraded trademark is the Ecological Footprint, arguably the best-known indicator in sustainability. Unfortunately, it's also in the *Oxford English Dictionary*, and by the time your slogan makes it there it belongs to the world. That's not always a bad thing, but if your innovation requires control over communications, quality, and brand, then a degraded trademark is a lost opportunity.

Copyright of your written materials, software, or music can protect the specific way you've expressed your creativity, but not the specifics of the ideas themselves, which can be redisseminated freely as long as specific pieces of language, computer code, or recordings aren't used. In cases where you wish to protect the ideas themselves, you have to step up to treating your IP as a trade secret, protecting it in contracts or patenting it. Trade secrets can be protected with simple language in a personnel manual or through other fairly straightforward procedures that make members of your team responsible legally for not disseminating key ideas. Contracts do the equivalent for people outside your organization.

Patents are one of the more stringent ways to protect IP but, paradoxically, have often been used to ensure that key IP remains broadly available. For example, a great way to keep an idea in the public domain is to patent it and then freely license it. (For a great case of this, check out the history of wheelchairs and the Physically Disabled Students Program in Berkeley in the 1960s.) Patents can be expensive but should be considered where control over your innovation is critical to your mission, to your success, or to eventual revenue generation.

Physical assets. These are the real-world, material things you need or can deploy to succeed. Do you need an office or a staging space for your innovation? Do you have free access to space as part of your hosting organization? Like Goodwill, do you have access to large amounts of contributed goods and services? Like the National Museum of the American Indian, is there a pre-existing trove of cultural artifacts and resources that will be folded into your innovation? Think hard about what's available to you that can help you launch, and write it down in the Key Resources box on the canvas.

Financial resources. Money is often critical to social sector start-ups but not always. Where will you get it? The traditional options include:

- *Individual donors.* This is usually where any social sector program starts, even if it's destined for government implementation. Some group of individuals or organizations pools its resources, meager or not, to pay for the early stages of the innovation. The money raised goes to travel, to research, and to hiring a staff person or two to anchor the effort. Many innovations remain primarily funded by individual donors, either a few writing big checks (upwards of $10,000 a year) or many, many smaller donors. A donor-funded innovation must very early identify donors as explicit targets and test against its hypotheses about their giving. A big advantage of getting money from donors is the flexibility they usually allow, which is very good for lean methodologies, and the learning that lean fosters is a great way to keep a community of donors engaged as you advance your innovation.

- *Foundations* are a great source of startup capital, but it remains to be seen how open they will be to the experimentation necessary in the lean startup. Restrictions on what a foundation will fund, what it *can* fund legally, and other factors may constrain your final service or product design. Traditionally, many foundations also become more prescriptive in their funding as a startup matures, demanding narrower, measurable program outcomes. Keep this in mind as you write them into your canvas!

- *Government.* With federal spending alone at almost $4 trillion a year, the government is far and away the largest funder of the social sector, and you should always consider whether your innovation is destined to be government-funded in the short, medium, and long run. (The National Museum of the American Indian was an example of a startup that was born of a privately funded initiative to make NMAI an integral part of the Smithsonian Institution.) There is a multitude of ways government funding may be part of your innovation, whether you're working within a government institution now, hoping to get a government grant or contract, or hoping to secure long-term funding for your innovation through legislative efforts.

Good will. Most social sector work is motivated *not* by financial gain but by social values, and the motivation behind those values is a major resource in the work. In the nonprofit sector, leaders are often acutely aware of "the case"—the charitable appeal of their work. There are "cases" that are likely to be widely held, like saving the environment or housing the indigent. Other cases may be vital to the general well-being, but will appeal to only a narrow demographic, like scientists who understand well before the general public the importance of a particularly narrow field of research. There are also "cases" that are contested in the public sphere to determine if they will become part of public policy, like healthcare. And there are "cases" that mobilize narrow constituencies to push programs into government, like certain forms of targeted subsidies.

Whatever the "case," the pool of good will is vital to any social innovation. It's a resource that can be cultivated as a way of generating almost every other resource on your list—money, volunteers, physical assets. As you begin to understand your social innovation, keep track of the kind of "case" it represents in the canvas.

Human resources. These resources include the staff, advisors, board members, and specific donors you need to succeed. Many times your human resources come to you, motivated by the cause or "case." Try to be intentional as well about the people you innovate with. Find people who've done pieces of what you're trying to do already and get them on board. Understand that it's OK to test your sense of whether a person is the right fit or not as soon as possible. The best way to find out is to ask them to jump in and perform right away. As an old saying goes: "The best work you'll ever get from someone is the work you get just before they get the job."

Table 4.5 Sample Key Resources

Smarter, Cleaner, Stronger	National Museum of the American Indian	Catalog Choice	New York City Toilet Bowl Retrofit
Strong coalition of dissemination partners	Huge legacy collection in New York State	Software design experience on team	Deep-pocketed public agency
The leading experts on the subject of climate/economy nexus	Strong congressional support	Support by environmental organizations with big lists	Large community of advocates in the plumbing community
Strong brand			

6. Partners

The Partners box on the canvas will be a bit of a moving target as you roll out your innovation, but start by thinking about the things that are essential to your innovation that you *don't* want to do yourself. Who can complement or augment your efforts? Who will the key members of your "ecosystem" be? Are they people or organizations you need to supply you with key resources? Are there strategic alliances that would increase your odds of success? Some of your partners may even get paid for their help. The word "partner" doesn't always imply complete alignment. Catalog Choice, for example, engaged with the Direct Marketing Association as part of its strategy—even though the DMA wasn't initially aligned with CC's goal of reducing throughput.

Table 4.6 Sample Partners

Smarter, Cleaner, Stronger	National Museum of the American Indian	Catalog Choice	New York City Toilet Bowl Retrofit
Large environmental organizations and lobbyists	George Heye Collection	Environmental organizations	Office of Management & Budget
State-based climate advocates	Key tribal leaders	US Postal Service	Low-flow toilet manufacturers
Local research institutions and economists	New York state legislature	Direct Marketing Association	Building owners associations

7. Revenue Streams

The Lean Change Canvas uses the social sector convention discussed in chapter 3 that funders are targets as well as customers. So if the questions appear customer-centric, it's because they are, but in the social sector context where the people who pay you are often not those you are directly serving. Try to avoid an "if-you-build-it-they-will-come" mentality here and think about organizations, government entities, and individuals who will definitely support you financially. As discussed earlier, there are four main sources of revenue in the social sector:

- *"Business" revenue.* Social sector organizations can make money virtually any way that businesses do, and common approaches include fees-for-service like admission fees, or tuition at a university, retail products like t-shirts for a school football team, plaintiff fees as a share of advocacy-related legal judgments, and referrals for people recruited for another entity. Like businesses, social sector organizations can sometimes generate their own revenue, and this capability can be a liberating force for innovation if it's possible.

- *Individual giving.* Many nonprofit organizations have large memberships that generate significant revenue, although such memberships are also often expensive to grow and maintain. Deep-pocketed individuals also play a critical role in supplying the liquidity and flexibility your organization needs to truly experiment.
- *Foundations.* As professionally staffed entities, foundations are great places to test your hypotheses with people who are somewhat expert in your field, but be careful because foundations also have little incentive to truly innovate and may not be a reliable barometer of your likely success.
- *Government funding.* This is a wide and deep pool of potential funding, including contracts, grant programs, and the potential for your innovation to be funded by legislative appropriation at the local, state, or national level.

What's the mix of these you expect? Make some estimates and fill out the canvas.

Table 4.7 Revenue Streams

Smarter, Cleaner, Stronger	National Museum of the American Indian	Catalog Choice	New York City Toilet Bowl Retrofit
Foundations	Congressional appropriations	Foundations	Capital funding from water bonds
Fees-for-service from larger environmental organizations	George Heye Trust	Premium service fees	Operating funds from water conservation budget
Key donors in relevant states	Admissions		
"Green" businesses in relevant states	Membership dues		
	Researcher access fees		

8. Key Activities

This is the box where you fill out the nuts and bolts of the day-to-day activities your innovation will entail. What will you be doing with your targets, including your funders, partners, and other key relationships? One goal of the hypotheses in this box is to figure out how to reduce your activities to the smallest possible amount that will drive the outcome you want. This "leaning down" may involve offloading activities or counting on partners for key parts of the work. But it should also start the process, discussed in greater detail later, of finding the minimum viable product—the very smallest step you can take to start making a meaningful difference.

Table 4.8 Key Activities

Smarter, Cleaner, Stronger	National Museum of the American Indian	Catalog Choice	New York City Toilet Bowl Retrofit
Research papers	Building construction	Website	Outreach to plumbers
Op-eds	Moving and managing the collection	Outreach/recruitment	Processing applications for reimbursement
Travel to states for briefings		Inventorying catalog vendors	
Cultivation of local experts	Repatriating remains		Monitoring and assessment
	Museum exhibits		
	Memberships		
	Research		

9. Expense Structure

Finally, take a stab at what your innovation will cost. Include staff and supplies/travel, but also how much key resources and all the activities identified earlier will cost. There is often a difference between the cost in the early stages, when you may be inventing your overall approach and running experiments, and later, when you've found a working model and have had time to hone it to a lean, mean operating model.

Table 4.9 Expense Structure

Smarter, Cleaner, Stronger	National Museum of the American Indian	Catalog Choice	New York City Toilet Bowl Retrofit
Research staff Travel	Capital expenses of building three facilities Operating expenses for three facilities Support for field presence on tribal lands	"Customer acquisition" through list sharing and purchases Web infrastructure	$200/toilet retrofit 10 percent administrative overhead

See P.51

All this work fits on one page in the form of the Lean Change Canvas. Some lean practitioners go one step deeper and create one- to two-page briefs for each box on the canvas. (See Steve Blank's great book, *The Startup Owner's Manual*, for more on what those can look like as well as some great checklists to consider as you move forward.) *□ Book Resource*

An even lighter approach is to prioritize the canvas in two stages—the right side, which should almost always be completed first, and the left side, which can be completed more incrementally as you gather data from work in the field. The right side comes first because the core of the lean startup is a focus on what your targets say and do, and the right side (Value Proposition, Targets, Relationships, Channels, and Revenue) are all about that. The left side of the canvas is more about what you will be doing in response to what you find out about your targets, so it can come a *Complete First* little later. The four sample canvases are available as completed in Resources.

Taken together, the Lean Change Canvas is where you set out your first comprehensive view or hypotheses about the innovation you are bringing to the world. It represents all the moving pieces of how you think you will make change happen, but many of the components will not be tested until after you've made sure that you've got a value proposition in the form of a product or service that really works for your targets and for the world.

The value of having all your hypotheses in one place is twofold. First, you may learn things as you launch that apply much later in the growth process, but you now have initial hypotheses that will let you examine these learnings further down the road. Second, and most important, you can start evaluating the interactions and tradeoffs of different parts of your operating model. For example, how much does your choice of how to implement change influence your revenue model? Does it increase or decrease the likelihood of being member-funded versus funded by foundations? These are not questions you need to resolve in the first weeks of your work, but the canvas gives you and your team a place to hold the multivariate experiment you are about to engage in!

Ask these?s

5

Discovery II:
Get Ready, Get Set ...

We're done with paperwork for a while now. The second part of discovery involves what lean practitioners call "getting out of the building," which means breaking the Plan–Fund–Do cycle by going directly to your targets (or customers, clients, funders ...). The core of discovery is testing your guesses with real people. In the next chapter, you'll test the "problem" hypotheses in your value proposition to make sure you understand what it is you're trying to change and how your targets themselves see the problem. Then you'll test your vision and the solutions you are proposing. But before you actually "get out of the building," you'll need to take some key preparatory steps to make sure you effectively encounter the people you hope will join you in making change happen.

Key Ingredients!

The process of discovery is one of radical doubt—you don't believe your guesses until you have validated them with customers. The lean startup is about a decade old as a practice in business, and in that time a few truisms have emerged that help practitioners be both visionary and grounded.

Honor Your Vision

You are starting a phase of direct contact with the world, with your targets, with those you hope to affect. There will be no shortage of naysayers and negative feedback if you are proposing true innovation. Know that by using the principles of the lean startup, you are giving your innovation the best shot at success, whether or not your initial formulation proves correct. Be ready to hear hard answers and to get useful feedback. Then remember that all of these are in the interest of giving your first impulse for change the best possible chance for success.

"No Plan Survives First Contact with Customers"

This truism from the private sector holds for the social sector as well. Your initial hypotheses and ideas about how the world worked as you envisioned it in the canvas are rarely right. Remember how the Homeless Services Center's first efforts focused on building community collaboration? It turned out that what was important was to focus on the amount of time each step toward a home was taking. It felt good to have disparate organizations helping each other out, but it wasn't the critical piece for solving the problem.

It's best to start with radical naivete, or what Buddhists call "beginner's mind." Don't be shy about asking questions about the problem or your proposed solutions. But be prepared to hear anything, and then to pivot to a new set of hypotheses based on your interviews.

Sometimes People Don't Know What They Need

As much as you should be listening to the people you will be interviewing, you may be exploring the creation of something that very few people understand at first. This truism comes from innovators as diverse as Steve Jobs (who once said, "A lot of times, people don't know what they want until you show it to them") and Paolo Freire (who built an entire theory around false consciousness and how people could embody the idea of their own oppression).

There is nothing elitist or unreasonable about innovation, about creating things that no one has seen before. So listen well during this discovery phase and gather evidence, but keep faith with your innovation until the conversations and hypothesis tests you've run tell you to shift direction. That too will undoubtedly happen on your way to success.

Know these — track them — be open to learn more

The Risks You Are Evaluating

In his book *Running Lean,* Ash Maurya usefully calls out three big categories of risk for startup companies:

- *Product risk,* which means the risks of making the product or service at the core of your innovation. Can you build the museum, get people's names from catalog lists, write great papers, get plumbers to retrofit toilet bowls? Sometimes this category is called *execution risk.*
- *Customer risk.* These are the risks around your targets. Can you reach and manage your funders? Will the people you are directly targeting (like newspaper editors) actually help you reach those you are indirectly targeting (like US senators)?
- *Market risk.* These are the "environmental" risks your whole effort faces. Will you be able to build an effective, funded, operational entity? Is there a good fit between the "case" for your innovation and the kinds of funders you need? For example, if you are counting on funding from a broad membership for a complicated or narrow cause, you may be in for some rough times.

You Need External Advice

Separate from the interviews that will constitute the core data for your hypothesis test, get some advice about your canvas and your hypotheses from some outside experts. Talk to at least two types of people—those who have tried to do something similar, and those whom you believe are likely to be "early adopters" of your innovation because they share so much of the same worldview. Explain that you will be testing hypotheses with a broad array of targets, "customers" and/or stakeholders, and have them take a critical look at the hypotheses you've generated so far. Whom do they recommend you speak with? What kinds of tests would they run on these hypotheses? Can they think of other hypotheses that you haven't thought of yet? Take all this great input to shorten the path to effective interviews in these two steps.

Identify/Review Big Risks

Do a gut check on where the biggest risks are for your innovation. What elements of your innovation make you most nervous?

Work from Falsifiable Propositions/Hypotheses

Your canvas has a number of hypotheses on it. As you work (usually from right to left across the canvas), think about how each hypothesis can be tested simply, resulting in a yes/no answer.

In the New York City Toilet Bowl Retrofit Program, for example, a major hypothesis was that plumbers would be willing to do retrofits. We could have asked plumbers unions and large contractors if they were interested, but a better test was to ask whether they would routinely conduct retrofits for $200 (or whatever price we thought was appropriate).

Even better would have been to put out a (nonbinding) Request for Inquiries (RFI) and to measure how many inquiries we got. Best practice today would be to put the RFI out online and measure the response rate at different price points (at $50, $100, and $200, for example).

Keep the Team Compact

You want to test your early hypotheses with a small team for a couple of reasons. First, you can't really outsource the kind of insight-gathering you're about to do. Your vision, your team's vision, must be tested by you, communicated as well and as directly as you can. And the feedback needs to come back to the source of the innovation—you—to effectively help the team learn.

The second reason for a compact team is that it is increasingly easy to test your hypotheses, so the leaner you can stay until you know the right direction the better. Staying lean in this phase means you can stay focused on learning and avoid building a team too early that may not fit where your innovation is headed. Your initial vision may, for example, be to build a strong door-to-door canvassing organization. After a few weeks of interviews and field-testing it may turn out that you'll be far more effective on the phone and that the early hiring of a canvassing expert leaves your effort with too much skill in one arena (canvassing) and too little where it counts (phone banking). *Innovation Accounting*

Finally, the sooner you figure out how to gather data cheaply the better off you'll be. One of the major frameworks of the lean startup is innovation accounting, a measure of how quickly you are actually innovating. We'll cover it more in chapter 11, but the more efficiently you can test, the quicker you'll learn and grow.

This bias toward lean-ness is increasingly pervasive in the private sector because of how many low-cost tools exist today for testing hypotheses. New companies today often need to demonstrate large-scale customer behaviors before they can raise any money from investors. Early investment in social sector innovation sometimes requires a lower threshold for hypothesis testing, but why spend a lot of money before you have at least an initial working model? Part of the idea behind the lean startup is to use scarce social sector resources more efficiently. Proving out your innovation in as lean a way as possible is the best way to do that.

Communicate

The lean startup needs you and all your partners in innovation (funders, bosses, boards, community members ...) to be open to the hard data that the discovery phase will generate. Regular communication about your hypothesis testing and your results will be critical to building a team that's ready to build, measure, learn, and pivot its way to unprecedented success.

Quality and Quantity

You will usually start with qualitative research (interviews and observation) about your hypotheses and then move on to testing your hypotheses with larger and larger numbers of targets. The important thing is to value *both* types of research. Insights from real discussions with real people are the most important, but they also have to start panning out in simpler interactions with more and more people. If your hypotheses aren't sustained when you start testing them quantitatively, it's time to regroup and find the paths forward that scale appropriately.

Early Evangelists

Some people will understand what you're about right away and love it. They are your most important targets, the people who somehow epitomize the problem you're trying to solve and the exact way you framed your solution. Spend a lot of time understanding what makes these folks true believers and what shapes their world. They will provide you with critical data for the first three stages of customer development.

Don't Let These Reasons Stop You!

Let's face it ... it's hard to talk to people. And it's even harder to have to listen to them not quite get your big idea. As teams prepare to "get out of the building" the darnedest reasons not to do so always seem to come up. To help inoculate you against this problem, here are some of the most common reasons for *not* interviewing people that we've heard over and over again. Read them here so you can dismiss them and move forward:

Know the Excuses then Just Do It!

- *"We can't talk to enough people to be statistically significant!"* Yes. That's the point. Nobody understands what you're doing yet, so getting a lot of them to listen could be hard. Try to get ten of them to agree with you and you'll be making progress. Another part of this objection is the focus on statistics, which are very important once you do start getting people to pay attention to your innovation. But until then, interviews give you rich details about why they aren't getting it, about what's not quite right for them, and about what makes them really interested.
- *"The foundation already approved the grant."* Sometimes you've already convinced a key target, a funder. Congratulations, but you owe it to yourself and the social problem you are taking on to give your innovation the best possible chance. Get out and talk to the people you are trying to serve so you can use the grant to the greatest effect.
- *"This is so obvious!"* Then your interviews will be short, but don't take it for granted that people just a little outside your inner circle may not think things are so clear. If they do, you'll move into implementation very quickly.
- *"We'll lose the element of surprise."* The most fundamental aspect of lean is learning, and worrying about the tradeoff between surprise and learning almost inevitably stifles the

learning and increases the negative surprises. And, as you'll see in the next section, you start by validating the problem, which doesn't reveal the solution to your early interviewees. You can be more selective with those you interview in the third step, the solution interviews.

- *"I don't want to raise expectations."* Sometimes, particularly in government, there's a fear that mentioning an innovation will create a demand that can't be met. This is usually in the category of problems you want to have. If there's that much demand, structure your interviews to document it and your odds of funding and adoption can only go up.

Be Ready for Success

Every once in a while, things come together and your innovation starts to take off beyond even your wildest dreams (for example, see the story of the Kony 2012 campaign in chapter 6). Take just a little time to plan how to handle expansion if your dreams come true.

Key Techniques for Outside the Building

The rest of discovery is about fearlessly testing your understanding of the problem and the key elements of your solution and then pivoting toward a product or service that definitely hits the mark. You do this testing by getting out and speaking with lots and lots of people. As your understanding grows, you can also use the Internet to test with more and more people, and in the process grow the list of early targets so vital to the next stages of customer development.

Interviewing is the core technique of the testing phase of discovery, and you can break the interview task in each step into three components.

1. Reach a Large Number of Interviewees

Generally, you and your team should aim to reach at least fifty people for each step. This is real work and, if you're lucky, will result in twenty to thirty in-depth interviews.

To get to this many people, start with the people you know and expand outward. Speak with direct targets (the people your product or service will interact with the most), with indirect targets (people you hope to reach through your direct targets), and with funders. You may find, with the latter group, that they are rarely approached for their view of problems and that they will welcome the chance to share how they see the space. You can further build the list by asking your first-level contacts for additional referrals ("Anyone else you know who works in this area/has this problem?"), cold-calling relevant people, and using social networks like LinkedIn or Facebook. Finally, develop a short script that gives your prospective interviewees a capsule understanding of what you are seeking to understand, and what they can hope to get out of taking the time to speak with you.

2. Conduct Effective Interviews

The key is to speak much less than you listen, and the most basic element of this is to ask open-ended questions (ones to which you can't answer yes or no). Rather than "Do you think you get too much junk mail?," ask "How much junk mail do you get?", or even "How do you feel about the different types of mail you get?" Beyond that, prepare a simple script that each member of your team follows to help with consistency in aggregating your results. Make sure your script leads your interviewee into an open discussion, that you capture key demographic information, that you tell a story that frames the interview, that you get key information about the environments they operate in (Who's the funding decision-maker? Where do they normally encounter this problem?, and so on), and that you or (preferably) a listening partner keep track of the data coming in with respect to your hypotheses.

There are two steps to take late in the interviews. First, after you've gotten good answers to open-ended questions, sometimes you can circle back around to your most basic hypotheses with very direct questions, like the "Do you get too much junk mail?" question above. Second, never miss the chance to learn more about the "environment" you're innovating into. Find out what else your targets do: their favorite museums, where they normally shop, whom they depend on for the best information. Use this as a chance to find out good metrics, too. Ask them who they know who's excellent in the space you're addressing, and what makes those people excellent. You can revisit these notes as you move into implementation and use them to set benchmarks for your own organization's performance.

3. Score or Evaluate the Interviews

Simple or complex, come up with the right scorecard for your particular customer development hypotheses and process. Figure 5.1 is a tool for doing this. Fill in the top row with things you want to measure and put each interviewee on one row. This grid will let you see which of your measures got the most positive (or negative) feedback in one place and can help you understand the spread (or diversity) of reactions to your innovation.

Online Testing and the Minimum Viable Product

Although not always possible, using online tools is another core technique to test the problem and the solution. In the early phases of an online approach, you run very simple online tests, like posting a webpage or a short video explaining the problem, then the solution, and then interviewing (by phone or in person) people who visit. But online testing is a vast world today, and it is

Figure 5.1 Interview Scorecard				
Interviewee	Reaction to Problem Statement 1	Reaction to Problem Statement 2	Reaction to Problem Statement 3	Excited? Urgent?
Interviewee 1				
Interviewee 2				
...				

This scorecard organizes reactions to problem statements 1, 2, 3 ...: Excited, Urgent Need, High Impact, Decision-Maker, and so on.

not uncommon for online startups in the for-profit world to run, with very few resources, dozens of tests a day once they start getting even very initial traction. In the social sector, this technique is most commonly found among political organizations in the runup to elections.

In lean practice, you use a minimum viable product to test both your problem hypotheses and your solution hypotheses. This is a very important concept with multiple variants, and we'll cover it in more depth in chapter 6.

Lean startups use customer development because that's how you ground-truth your guesses ... with the people you hope to influence, to serve, to raise money from, to inspire. It's time to meet them ... first contact!

6

Discovery III:
Get Out of the Building!

Test the Problem

You don't start by testing whether people love your ideas. You start by testing to find out whether you understand their problems. Think about why you are innovating. What thing in the world are you trying to fix, and for whom? Stop right there and start testing your guesses about that. You are done with this step when:

1. You know who your targets are, and
2. You understand the problem from your targets' point of view.

"Get Out of the Building" means that you will achieve this understanding through direct contact with people. Chapter 5 discussed how to reach a large number of people for interviews, and even if you do a lot of your problem testing online with an MVP, you must have some face-to-face contacts to be sure you understand, at a human level, what's really going on with your targets.

In the problem interviews or MVP, present your problem hypothesis. Ideally, you do so as part of your interview sequence or your discussion. If it's a direct problem for your target, more often than not you won't need to say much or show much. They will be directly engaged with it already. Table 6.1 provides examples of statements from "engaged" customers.

Table 6.1 Sample Statements of Enthusiasm

Case Study	Hypothetical Response from an Engaged Customer
National Museum of the American Indian	"I can't believe the Smithsonian has been hiding the remains of almost 20,000 Native Americans. What are they going to do to make this right?"
Catalog Choice	"I'm tired of having to throw away half the paper I get in my mailbox."
Toilet Bowl Retrofits	"Wait … the city is going to *pay me* to put in new toilet bowls?"
Smarter, Cleaner, Stronger	"If you environmentalists knew how to talk to businesspeople, we'd be further down the road for sure."

If your targets don't engage fully with your problem questions, you can use what Steve Blank calls a *problem presentation* (see Table 6.2). Fill out a table with a few different ways of describing the problem. On each line add the ways the problem is being addressed today and finally list some of the ways your solution will address them. You can make a slide or draw it on a wall, starting by unveiling the "Problems" column first. Then listen!

The second column ("Today's Solutions") is valuable because it gives you a sense of how your targets are solving the problem today. What kind of steps are they taking now? Is your list of existing solutions accurate? How much attention are targets putting into existing solutions? Start out where your proposed solution fits and how it is already happening in the world.

Problem Presentation Table

Table 6.2 Blank Problem Presentation

Problems	Today's Solutions	Proposed Solutions
1	. . .	. . .
2	. . .	. . .
3	. . .	. . .

At this stage, either don't show or don't emphasize column 3 ("Proposed Solutions"). These will be changing as a result of new understandings you gain in this step of testing the problem you're addressing.

Online Problem Testing

If a significant part of your innovation will be delivered online (on the Web or via personal computers or cellphones), you should get online as soon as possible to test your problem there. You don't need to know how to build software or even webpages to do this. A list of easy-to-use resources is available at www.leanchange.net/resources/MVP.

You can start with a series of text messages, a simple webpage, or a blog that presents the problem, you can post a video or short narrated slideshow or animation, or you can circulate Web-based surveys. Any of these give you something against which to gauge your targets' reaction. Even cooler, you can test different

The Five Whys: Why Senators Won't Vote for Action on Climate Change

Why?
- Because their constituents don't care about climate change

Why?
- Because climate change isn't connected to their lives

Why?
- Because climate change doesn't seem to have much to do with the things they do every day

Why?
- Because making a living seems unrelated to climate change

Why?
- Because the connection between climate action and jobs/economic growth isn't clear

Figure 6.1 The Five Whys
Another good way to deepen your problem interviews is to follow the Lean technique of the Five Whys. As you seek to understand a problem, keep asking "But why?" about the source of the problem until you've gone down five layers of causality.

ways of presenting the problem, randomizing who sees which description and gauging which problem statement is most on the money. (Online, the generic name for this kind of testing is "A/B testing.") Whichever approach you choose to test the problem online, this approach is called your low-fidelity MVP—it's the simplest description of the problem you're trying to solve that allows you to get the insights you need.

An Online "Problem Test"
(Low-Fidelity MVP) for Catalog Choice

The possibilities for using digital resources for testing your problem hypothesis are endless. Just remember to ground them with face-to-face interviews as well since these interviews help you make sure that you are validating the actual impact directly.

Look for at least three types of information as you conduct your interviews and tests. First, do your targets *agree* with your problem hypothesis? Are they confirming it, or modifying it, or not even recognizing it as a problem? When they get an email with the problem in the title line, do they open it?

Second, *how strongly* do your targets feel about the problem? Do they acknowledge it without any strong interest, or are they worked up and/or already taking action on it? Does it drive how they vote, where they live, how they spend money? If you're

Figure 6.2 An Online Problem Test

testing online, you can even give them a chance to sign up for your solution. If they do, you have good data on their degree of interest, and you can politely respond to them that you'll get back to them very soon (which you will, in the next step!).

Third, can you identify the specific circumstances that lead to the problem? Is there a series of events that is repeatedly associated with the problem you are trying to solve? A clear understanding of the context in which the problem occurs helps by both opening up the possibility for a wider array of solutions (tied to some additional causal element you've identified) and by creating a repeatable pattern that may help your innovation really take hold.

When are you done with testing the problem hypothesis? When you have a clear signal from your interviews, your online tests, and your whole team that your view of what's wrong in the world jibes with the experience of your most critical targets.

When you are at that point, bring your team together and review the evidence you've gathered. It's highly unlikely that your initial vision couldn't do with some tweaking to better fit the data you've gotten directly from the diverse targets you've interviewed, observed, and interacted with. So do some tweaking,

---

How to Get Lots of People for Online Tests

There are two main approaches to recruiting people online, push and pull. In push models you use lists that you get from your existing network (their online communities, for example) or that you pay for. In pull models, you seed the world with connections back to your online site with things like public events that garner press attention (earned media), press releases, blog entries, and Google, Twitter, and Facebook ads (which can be tightly targeted and therefore efficient).

revisit your Lean Change Canvas, and update your hypotheses based on what you've learned. You've just completed your first pivot.

Test the Solution

Congratulations! Your innovation is about to be born!

This is it: the time you start pushing your ideas out into the world, out of the building, and into the arms of the people you're trying to affect.

Start very small. Start very, very small. Remember Steve Blank's advice: "You want to build something that barely works, but if you took it away from people they'd beg to pay you for it."

Since he said that to me in 2008, the lean startup movement has defined even more minimal ways of testing solutions. The low-fidelity MVP was all about getting insights into the targets' views of the problem you're trying to solve. Because we're moving from testing the problem hypotheses to testing the solution hypotheses, the tool we'll use is called the *high-fidelity MVP* and, as you'll see, even if it doesn't work at all, it can be a great test of your solution hypotheses.

The goal in solution testing is to deploy your solution with the smallest possible product or service that still provides a good test of your solution hypotheses. You want, in particular, to test two dimensions of your solution. From the Value Proposition and Targets boxes on your Lean Change Canvas, you want to test whether the product or service solves the problem you targeted in step 2 and for the right people. You also want to start drawing from the Relationships hypotheses, in particular to test how you will be "getting" your targets. Eric Ries calls these the *value hypothesis* and the *growth hypothesis*, respectively.

These two dimensions are closely related to the online marketing concept of virality, which is worth considering even if you don't expect your innovation to rely on virality. Like the spread of disease viruses, virality has two critical dimensions. First, is the solution infectious? When a person encounters it, does it stick? Do they "get the bug"? If you take it away from them, what will they do to get it back? This is another way to understand your test of solution hypotheses and the infectiousness of your innovation. The strength of your targets' adoption of your solution is a key measure of this "infectiousness."

The second dimension of virality is contagion, or how widely and quickly the solution spreads. This is measured by things like how likely your targets are to discuss the innovation with their peers, in person, or virtually by email, by using a tool, like sharing on LinkedIn, or in publications like blog posts. You want to understand if and how they will share the solution with a number of their peers and whether they will be good channels to propagate your innovation if it works. Here you are starting to answer the hypotheses you have about targets and about your relationships to them, in particular your "get" hypotheses. Ideally, the minimum viable product tests both dimensions.

Time to Get Agile: The Minimum Viable Product

Principle 3 of the lean startup is agile development, and solution testing is where it starts to come into full play. In *The Lean Startup,* Eric Ries defines the MVP as "the fastest way to get through the Build–Measure–Learn feedback loop with the minimum amount of effort." In practice, this means that the MVP can be much less than the product or solution you envision. As long as it starts to test your hypotheses about the value proposition and, if possible, your relationships to targets, it's a splendid start.

The MVP is the beginning of the Build–Measure–Learn cycle that is the central way you move forward in the lean startup. From here on out, every change you make to your innovation

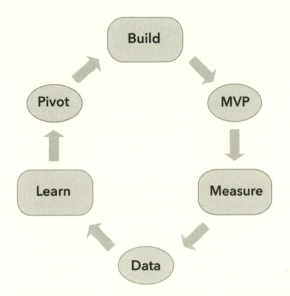

Figure 6.3 Build-Measure-Learn Loop for the Minimum Viable Product

and/or every part of your Lean Change Canvas should be driven as a result of having "built" a change, measured its impact, and learned its lessons. Now, for the very first contact of your solution hypotheses with your targets, there are lots of ways to go.

In the "Smarter, Cleaner, Stronger" project we ran at Redefining Progress there were all three types of targets: direct (newspaper editors), indirect (US senators), and funders (large climate advocacy organizations trying to muster Senate votes). In effect, we produced an MVP for each of them. We had national reports on the economic benefits of climate action, so we sent copies of those to editors in local markets of swing states and measured their interest in the generic research as a proxy for their undoubtedly stronger interest in research local to their market. We set preliminary meetings between businesspeople and some of the senators we were targeting to see how they would respond in the

Table 6.3 High-Fidelity MVP/Tests for Case Studies

Case Study	MVP	Specific Solution Hypothesis
National Museum of the American Indian	A signup list for researchers (DT) interested in using the collection	The research community would use a national collection
	Letters from tribal leaders (IT) calling for the museum	NMAI at least partially addresses the problem of repatriating remains
	Meetings with key senators (F)	Congress will fund a new museum
Smarter, Cleaner, Stronger	Send press release about available research to newspaper editors (DT)	Editors care about economic benefits of climate action
	Have business leaders seek meetings with senators (IT)	Senators will listen to businesspeople about climate change
	Ask for funding from large climate advocacy organizations (F)	Advocates will fund the research to influence Senate votes
Catalog Choice	A signup webpage for consumers—see Figure 6.2 (DT)	Consumers want this service
	No Indirect Targets	
	Set up meeting with foundations (F)	Foundations will pay for Catalog Choice, at least initially
Toilet Bowl Retrofits	Request for inquiries from plumbers interested in retrofits posted (DT)	Plumbers looking to perform retrofits
	Interviews with landlords and property owners (IT)	Property owners will welcome free water-saving retrofits
	Ask for funding for a pilot project from the city's Office of Management & Budget, New York City (F)	OMB will allow retrofit funding under bonding authority

DT: Direct Target; IT: Indirect Target; F: Funder

meetings and what kinds of issues came up. Finally, we asked national environmental groups if they would pay us to do state-specific reports (they had already paid us for the national versions).

MVP Types

The most basic high-fidelity MVP takes everything you know and have learned through your interviews and pares your innovation down to the most basic element possible. What is the simplest thing you can offer that addresses the problem you explored in step 2? Remember, this is not necessarily the thing you envisioned when you decided to launch the innovation. It should now be informed by real contact with real targets, and then pared down to be an MVP.

We started with what we already had, national reports, and were able to test the viability of state-specific reports *before* we had produced state-specific research. As a result, we got funding and developed a coalition of national organizations that included labor unions and several large climate advocacy groups working to move our research into the mainstream.

Table 6.3 shows sample MVPs for each of our case studies, as well as the specific hypothesis, in the rightmost column, that is being tested with that MVP. In many social sector projects, the disconnect between who pays for and who receives the innovation means that each of these targets may require, as in the case we just discussed, a slightly different MVP. But don't worry. As the results flow in, you will be increasingly unifying these MVPs into a single operating model that optimizes all these relationships.

Each box in Table 6.3 describes an MVP for that target category, as well as, in parentheses, the kind of target. Note that the MVP doesn't always test for the full solution hypothesis. It simply needs to test for the first hypothesis that generates learning and suggests answers that can lead to a full-blown solution.

A blog post. In 2009, after two years of abuse by a fellow Tufts student, Wagatwe Wanjuki started a blog, "Raped at Tufts University," and women at several campuses followed suit within a couple of years with blogs and, in at least one case, a Tumblr. Each of these simple products successfully became major resources for women on their respective campuses facing an epidemic of unreported campus sexual violence. In 2013, a national organization, End Rape on Campus (EROC), was formed to respond systemically to the needs of rape survivors. Among other services, they coordinate Title IX suits that hold campuses accountable for education, prevention, and remedies.

In this case, the MVP for education, prevention, and redress was a blog post. Wagatwe put it out there and thousands of women responded. She had proven the solution hypothesis that silence was a huge problem, and, over time, that evolved into a full-service advocacy organization (EROC).

A blog post is easy to implement (though it may be hard to write a great one!), and it allows both a test of the solution hypothesis and also of the spread of the solution. By watching how much the blog is reposted (or "liked" on Facebook and similar indicators) and to whom, you can start to get a good idea of the scale of change possible with your innovation.

A short video. The most notorious video MVP is probably the one for Dropbox, a software product that automatically synchronizes your files across different devices. Claiming that the service would launch in three months, Drew Houston, an MIT undergraduate at the time, designed a self-narrated series of screenshots that, on the surface, seemed very simple and made the product look as if it were already operating. Below the surface, the video was chock-full of puns and insider jokes that reached enthusiastic early adopters ("earlyvangelists" in Steve Blank's

> *Kony 2012: Impact Figures*
>
> - 5 million tweets in the first week
> - 100 million views in the first six days—a record
> - 58 percent of young adults had heard about the video within four days
> - 1.4 million Twitter mentions in the first three days
> - 13,536 percent increase in viewership after Oprah tweeted about the video

terminology). Within two days the number of people who had signed up for this yet-to-appear product had grown by over 1,500 percent. Dropbox took over 18 months to actually launch, but by then Drew had secured the funding needed to meet the pent-up demand. This MVP is one of the most studied in the lean world and is a great reference point if you're looking to go this route.

On March 5, 2012, Invisible Children launched a new video entitled "Kony 2012" that easily dwarfed Dropbox's effort. Within a week, it was viewed by over 100 million people. The video was an MVP for a broader campaign to make its subject (a warlord who fueled his army with child soldiers) globally infamous and to pressure US action against him.

Unfortunately, Invisible Children wasn't "ready for success." Within a few days, the American star of the video cracked under the social pressure and was even arrested for public nudity. This news, although not quite as widespread as the video itself, significantly undermined its long-term impact. Nevertheless, the video played a critical role[1] in President Obama's decision to send military advisors to aid in capturing the warlord. As of this writing, though, he has not been caught.

---

1 See, for example, www.theguardian.com/news/datablog/2012/apr/20/kony-2012-facts-numbers?newsfeed=true#zoomed-picture.

Ads (online and off). Why actually do something when you can just say you're doing it? That's the general principle behind an advertising-based MVP, and it seems to consistently rub people the wrong way. For many situations, though, it's actually ethical and makes a lot of sense.

You may already have done a version of this for your low-fidelity MVP. You make a landing page for your innovation that lays out the problem and elements of the solution you're proposing. (If you don't have a website, get a free phone number from Google Voice and record an appropriate message.) Then advertise:

- *Virtually,* using ads on Facebook, Google, and other websites and services. Because the most effective online advertising platforms today use an auction system, the better your sense of your targets, the more inexpensive such advertising becomes. You generally pay on a "cost-per-click" or CPC basis, which means that you pay only when someone clicks on your ad. More targeted ads can actually cost less if there are few people trying to deliver your particular message to your particular targets. An online ad lets you immediately measure the appeal of your solution and do so at a scale limited only by your budget.
- *In newspapers and similar local media.* An effort by New American Media (NAM) to recruit teachers of color started by convening publishers of ethnic newspapers to design an ad for their own communities, killing multiple birds with one stone. Rather than directly recruiting the teachers, NAM was able to get local community leaders (the publishers of the very papers they were using for their campaign) to help them target specific people with specific messages.
- *With leaflets and posters.* An age-old organizing technique: put up a poster, hand out some flyers, and see who shows

up. That flyer is an MVP—a series of problem and solution statements designed to reach your targets. When the flyer adds "bring your friends," it's testing not just the solution but the channels and relationships hypothesis.

Whether you are getting people to click on ads, go to a website or call a number they read about in the paper, or come to an in-person meeting based on a flyer they've received, the next step for this MVP is to deliver at least a statement about the solution you have drawn your targets in to learn about.

The ad-based MVP delivers data on both the value and the growth hypotheses.[2] For the value, or solutions hypothesis, you can creatively test variants on your solution, as illustrated in the two sample Google AdWords ads in Figure 6.4. You can also test the spread of your innovation by monitoring how many targets heard of it by directly seeing the "ad" and how many were told about your solution by other people ("virally").

Remember one of the fundamentals of the lean revolution: the ability for organizations to know faster than ever before whether what they are trying is having the intended impact or not. The ad-based MVP is probably closest in implementation to age-old organizing techniques, and even for that model this

Figure 6.4 Sample Online Ads

---

2 This is A/B testing. See www.leanchange.net/resources#AB for a list of resources for this kind of testing.

change is revolutionary. If you are willing to take all the data you can now collect (email addresses and activity, Twitter/Facebook/Instagram/LinkedIn activity plus Snapchat/Tumblr/Vines permissioned information about people's locations) as seriously as the traditional stuff (who shows up, who returns your phone calls, who volunteers), you will be part of the next, wildly effective wave of organizing.

The concierge MVP, a.k.a. "do it by hand." A concierge at a hotel offers guests personal service. A concierge MVP replaces as many as possible of the mechanisms and processes you envision in your solution with handholding, personal service.

Meena Palaniappan already had a huge network, deployed technology, and three years' experience in the complex world of supplying water to the destitute slums of Indonesian cities. She founded Atma to design software that would codify the lessons she'd learned in service of the bottom of the economic pyramid.

She hopes to crowdsource this information using mobile phones, enticing a network of "reporters" to share information across the communities and help people find the highest-quality water at the lowest prices. At the same time, she could use the data to show the formal water utilities exactly how much they could make by installing pipes, sewers, and essential sanitation infrastructure.

Rather than starting with a mobile app with lots of moving parts, a concierge MVP looks for the most basic way to handhold your way to a solution. Think about how many hypotheses are being implicitly tested when you launch an application on a mobile phone, particularly in places where there is not yet deep penetration of smartphones and/or computers. Assuming that the solution hypothesis is 100 percent correct (in this case, that transparency about water prices and water quality would save residents significant money and improve their health), success still depends on whether the software works and is well designed, whether the right people (eager participants/early adopters) have the right phones or any phones at all, and a range of other factors.

A concierge MVP for Atma could be as basic as running the same process using flyers or posters that would be distributed daily to local residents. Meena had already done tremendous customer discovery, and she had found real demand for this information in the form of community organizations and leaders eager to see her idea launch for their communities. She therefore had no shortage of human infrastructure committed to the project's success.

The concierge approach might simply ask key residents to call in the information about price and quality every day to a central person. Then that person could print a small flyer or a series of small posters and go out and distribute them to the targeted communities. The delivery mechanism would be very simple and in a form residents understood well—written on paper. Using such a simple system, Meena could test the value hypothesis (did water pricing go down and did quality go up?) and her growth hypotheses about how many people would report prices in, how many would use the information to buy water differently, and whether there was a business model that scaled enough to drive the utility into action.

Water is an essential part of life in the slums where Meena works, and one that residents could not take for granted, so such a manual test would work unambiguously or not at all. As more and more people started reporting water data and as they started using that data and understanding its value, Atma could build offerings to keep up with demand. Those offerings would eventually become integral to the mobile app that was the intended delivery mechanism all along. A mobile application can change everything, but its simplicity and ease can be simulated for short periods with simple, human mechanisms. It's better to know that the core innovation is vital before you invest scarce resources in building software or any other more expensive infrastructure.

You have now collected a lot of data and tested your most important hypotheses about the problem you're trying to solve and the innovative solution you are trying to launch. The final stage of discovery is evaluating it all and deciding if you've failed fast, if you are ready to proceed, or ...

7

Discovery IV:
Pivot, Proceed, or Quit

When is solution testing over? The end of solution testing and of the entire discovery phase comes when one of three things happens:

1. You Haven't Found a Solution That Works for Enough of the People You Are Trying to Reach

Congratulations, you've failed fast! Undoubtedly you were trying to solve a difficult social problem, and, as we've discussed, that problem may be so serious that it *has* to be solved sooner or later. (Failure may not, in fact, be an option.) The lean startup process helped you figure out faster than ever before that your approach *wouldn't* work, preserving human and financial capital for the next run at the problem. You've tried and you've learned, and, most important, you have not wasted resources that are still vitally needed in the search for solutions.

2. You've Run Out of Resources

Sometimes you run out of critical resources before you've given your solution a fair shake. You run out of money because funders don't see the value of your innovation yet. Key people (your partners, even you) burn out or have a hard time accepting interim failures that crop up (like first contact with customers). Partners that are core to your plan pull back for their own reasons.

The practice of lean startups has a measure for itself called *innovation accounting*, which measures learning per dollar, or how many solution tests you can run for a given investment of time and money. If you run truly lean using this method, you will get further toward understanding your problem and testing solutions than with any other method by far. We'll discuss innovation accounting and the patterns of resource use that can get you a longer "runway" in more depth in chapters 8 through 11.

Starting anything new involves real risk, but without risk taking there would never be the kind of change we need to make the world a better place. The more we can keep that in mind, the more we will value change-makers who are trying true innovation in service of their causes. Equally important, the less we stigmatize failure in the service of innovation the more creativity we will engender. And that creativity will be efficient, honestly and rapidly evaluating its own success, preserving vital capital for the next approaches to our society's thorniest problems.

3. You Are Ready to Move Forward!

Your testing in the customer discovery phase showed that you've identified a genuine problem and a solution that can be implemented in a way that works for people (your targets). You are at this point because you've answered yes to three key questions:

A. Does Your Solution Solve a Problem for Your Targets (Value Hypothesis)?

Your vision of the problem was validated and your innovation solved that problem through relationships and channels that were robust and predictable. In the private sector this is called "product/market fit," and it usually means that your innovation is flying off the shelves. Even in the social sector, this is the kind of enthusiasm you should be looking for before you proceed. What does that kind of enthusiasm look like?

It means that a significant fraction of those who encountered your innovation had no reservations at all about it. They wanted it yesterday, and in exactly the form you presented it. Table 7.1 gives examples of the kinds of statements you should have heard from a significant fraction of the targets you engaged, as well as some sample statements that are just shy of enthusiastic.

This "just shy" category is probably the most important one to evaluate carefully. If your targets are *conditionally* enthusiastic, think carefully about whether you've adequately tested your solution hypothesis. The conditions your interviewees are placing on your innovation may be simple to accommodate, but more often than not they represent an inadequate conceptualization of the problem and/or solution on your part. You may not want to proceed fully unless you flesh out a solution that puts the pieces together in a way that feels ready to go as is to your targets.

Statements like these can be graded on a quantitative scale (such as 1 to 5, with 5 being most enthusiastic). You'll want a preponderance of the people you interviewed or tested to be high on that scale (rating 4s or 5s).

Many innovations in the social sector today can be tested online, and it's possible to get a very granular understanding of how people are reacting to your solution using the vast array of online tools that are now available. Some of these tools are listed at www.leanchange.net/testtools.

Table 7.1 Enthusiastic Statements and Those That Are Not

Case Study	Typical "Enthusiastic" Statement (Target)	"Just Shy" of Enthusiastic Statement (Target)
National Museum of the American Indian	"It is totally unacceptable for Native remains to languish any longer, unaccounted for in dismal vaults. We have to move forward with a proper institution, the National Museum of the American Indian." (US senator, or senior tribal leader)	"My research would benefit greatly from a new museum as long as its collections were fully digitized." (researcher)
Catalog Choice	"How can I sign up?" (junk mail recipient)	"It would be so cool if I could turn catalogs on and off depending on the time of year." (junk mail recipient)
Toilet Retrofits	"When can I start doing retrofits?" (plumber)	"What kind of paperwork is involved in getting paid?" (plumber)
Smarter, Cleaner, Stronger	"Can you send more information to the business editor today?" (newspaper editor)	"Let me check our publication schedule to see if we have space in the next few weeks." (newspaper editor)

B. Do You Know Who Your Targets Are and How to Reach Them in Sufficient Numbers (Growth Hypothesis)?

A second key component of moving on is that you've validated at least some hypotheses about who you are targeting with your innovation and how you will reach them. In the Lean Change Canvas these hypotheses sit in the "Relationships" box and the "Channels" box, and they constitute your model of how to get, keep, and grow your targets (or customers).

You tested these hypotheses by seeing how many and what kinds of people clicked on your online ad, watched your video, or came to the meetings you advertised with posters all over town. For funding targets, you have a sense of how many "asks" you have to make to get a committed individual donor, how many phone calls to foundations result in meetings, how receptive elected officials are to loosening the purse strings on public funding.

It's not just enough to know that people want your innovation. You need a sense of how you are going to deliver it to them and get what you need back from them, whether that's money, engagement, or change. You are ready to move past customer development when you know that your innovation stands a good chance of reaching enough targets to achieve the change you are aiming for.

The work of figuring this out is far from over. In some ways, this first phase of customer development, discovery, is primarily about testing and honing your solution. You need to validate how you will reach targets here as well, but phase two of customer development, validation, focuses almost completely on fleshing out the growth hypotheses.

C. Can You Fund Your Innovation?

The eventual availability of funding at this early stage needs to be an obsession—but it can also be a distraction. Remember that in the social sector the people or interests you are serving are usually *not* the ones funding you. So a critical third question for social sector innovation is whether or not there is a sustainable way to fund your solution.

In private sector startups, getting paid is one of the key ways you can test your solution hypothesis: Have you solved enough of a problem that someone is willing to pay you for your solution? In ideal cases, you find customers (or targets) who are *already* paying something for an alternative way of solving their problem.

A significant fraction of social sector innovations do end up collecting revenue from their targets. Museums, hospitals, state parks, and private and some public schools are all examples of social sector products and services that charge at least something for their use. Innovations within and around such institutions can test for their targets' willingness to pay by adding a fee-for-service component. Short of that, you can get some sense of that willingness to pay by surveying existing and paying users about what they are likely to be willing to contribute.

Even in these cases, though, the full cost of the government or nonprofit initiative is rarely covered by the program's beneficiaries. That's why your solution testing in this phase needs to test your value hypothesis with potential sources of revenue. Does your innovation solve a problem that a set of foundations or corporate philanthropies find important? Is it likely that elected officials and/or government agencies will sponsor your program at scale? Are there existing grant or funding programs that your program or service will qualify for? Are you likely to serve a large enough constituency that funders will see your efforts as worthwhile?

All these questions should be answered with real data in the form of conversations with program officers, invited proposals, or at least clear expressions of interest in your innovation should it prove out over the next few months. Answering this question in the affirmative at this stage will always be a judgment call. Do the funders you have in mind (individuals, members, foundations, government, corporations) usually fund initiatives like this? Sometimes your solution may not fit the usual models. How open are potential funders to unconventional solutions to the problems they care about? Are there specific components that you know they've already ruled out (like lobbying, scholarships, or buildings)?

But the question of funding can be a distraction as well. The question of when to seek funding and how much intersects with one of the central tenets of the lean startup—the ease with which it is now possible to know if what you're doing is working. In Silicon Valley today, it is almost impossible to raise significant funds for a startup *before* the next phase in customer development (validation). The threshold there is that not only must you have a compelling and proven value proposition ("compelling" in business means it can make significant money), you must have a partially proven model for your "Get–Keep–Grow" funnel. You need real data with real people in real interaction with a version of your product or service.

In case this level of proof seems onerous, the alternative can often be worse: absent proven customer behavior, you receive investment without really knowing how much, eventually, your company may be worth and how much it will take to be successful. And this lack of shared understanding can set you up for significant conflict down the line with your investors.

In the social sector, I suggest you follow a similar practice wherever possible. If you start with a greater emphasis on testing your ideas than on raising funds (that is, if you start with ends rather than means), when the time comes to raise money you can go to funders with a clear picture of where you're headed in terms of impact. They can join you on a journey that will certainly involve twists and turns, but informed by a framework that you have built and shared with them. Their investment is then a way of joining you on the lean path forward.

Let's face it: all entrepreneurs, whether for-profit or for-benefit, take risks and make personal sacrifices for their cause. If you happen to fail fast, then you've still done well by yourself and your cause. You've preserved the most vital capital of all—yourself—and your ability to move on and to innovate again.

On the other hand, you may be showing promising results. The longer you can stretch out the time between when you start to test your innovation and when you have to lock in a specific set of practices and performance that's driven by investors or funders, the more likely it is you'll find the most effective, most innovative approaches to the problem you're tackling. Overall, it's still too early in the customer development process to be certain of your revenue. You can continue to explore funding sources as you move forward.

Conclusion

You leave the discovery stage when:

1. You failed fast.
2. You run out of resources.
3. You've proven your problem and solution hypotheses, found some great targets, and have started to raise money.

Remember Monica and Santa Cruz's Homelessness Services Center? There was a moment, about a year into their new program, when it became clear that they weren't going to get anywhere near their target number (180) of people transitioned into new housing. They hadn't really failed, because they had gotten 20 people housed. They hadn't run out of money, mostly because they were funding their initiative out of existing resources deployed differently toward this goal. They had amply proven their problem hypothesis (that few if any homeless people were being placed in permanent homes), but their solution hypothesis (that community partnerships and increased community and landlord good will would accelerate placement) wasn't panning out.

They did the hard thing at this point. Instead of moving forward, knowing full well that they would never reach their goals, they pivoted. And this is actually the most common outcome of a healthy discovery phase.

The easy thing would have been to just continue to trickle along, to keep telling themselves, the community, and their donors that they were innovating, that they had a bold goal and would get as close as possible. Next easiest would have been to quietly shutter the efforts—to acknowledge failure and go back to business as usual.

The hard thing? The hard thing was to take an honest look at *why* the program wasn't working and to develop some new solution hypotheses. In doing so, HSC moved away from the familiar terrain of collaborative, community-based work to a focus on a nuts-and-bolts bureaucratic process that's been driving unprecedented results. The one they settled on, reducing the time between eligibility and lease-signing, enabled them to ruthlessly comb the system for inefficiencies and make progress. One result was to shave the placement time from 160 days to 45.

By the time you get to a pivot point, you've come close to failure and you may be close to running out of money. You may even have found a "pretty good" solution and touted it to your biggest funders. It takes real courage to sum up all the hard truths about these experiments, to reject your own best guesses, and to feel like you're going backward, back into the discovery phase. But in fact, pivoting is the only sustainable way of moving forward.

How do you perform a pivot? At some point, while you are rigorously evaluating your solution hypothesis, have a meeting with your team specifically geared toward making a pivot decision. Reexamine your Lean Change Canvas and push really hard on the assumptions in it to creatively reshape them in ways you think, this time around, will be even more effective at driving the results you seek.

Table 7.2 shows examples of a range of pivot types, and you may want to keep it handy for that meeting. It's meant to help you think creatively about types of pivots that could work for your situation.

Table 7.2 Pivot Types and Examples

Pivot Type	Description and Example
Zoom-in	Zoom-in pivots occur a lot in legislative campaigns: the product or service is narrowed down from the original conception to just a piece of the original vision.
Zoom-out	You find that initial vision isn't enough and you expand the offering. For example, antirecidivism programs may discover that counseling has to be supplemented with income support as well.
"Customer" Segment	The vision may be good, but you find a different set of customers (a.k.a. direct, indirect, or funder targets). For example, it turns out that the users of a museum with a sliding-scale admissions program are unusually generous, making foundations less essential as targets than originally planned.
Customer Need	Because you got to know your targets so well, you figured out something they needed even more than your original offering. Literacy programs in impoverished communities are notorious for transforming themselves into nutrition programs because it turns out that, once their bellies are full, low-income kids are eager to learn.
Outcome-to-Capacity	In the process of innovating for a specific cause, you discover a mechanism that is useful more broadly. Move-on.org started as an anti-impeachment campaign during the Clinton administration before becoming a powerful tool for a wide range of advocacy outcomes.

Table 7.2 Pivot Types and Examples (*cont.*)

Pivot Type	Description and Examples
Capacity-to-Outcome	The reverse of outcome-to-capacity. An organization may start with the intention to build a capacity, like electoral power, and end up focused on a particular outcome, like education reform. Example: Californians for Justice.
Intensity	Sometimes you start out to deliver high-quality, intense services to a limited population, but, in an intensity pivot, shift to a program with lower intensity and far greater reach. The converse can also happen.
Funding	You start out with one way to fund your innovation and shift to another—for example, shifting from foundation funding to fee-for-service.
Engine of Growth	The focus of this pivot is your growth hypothesis—you change the way in which you try to expand the number of targets you can reach to be even more effective. An example of a growth pivot is a move from email campaigns to social media campaigns.
Channel/Pathway	You choose a completely different route to your targets. For example, a union might choose to shift its organizing from within the workplace to organizing by neighborhood or by finding workers within a sector but outside of their workplace.
Technology	You find a better mousetrap—a shift in the technique or technology you use to deliver the innovation. This is a good pivot to consider if you're already well established and can raise the capital to invest in the shift from a proven, loyal base of existing targets.

Source: Partly adapted from Eric J. Ries, *The Lean Startup: How Today's Entrepreneurs Use Continuous Innovation to Create Radically Successful Businesses* (New York: Crown, 2011).

Figure 7.1 summarizes the whole flow of discovery from problem testing through pivoting.

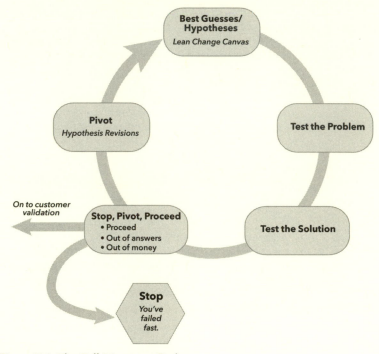

Figure 7.1 The Full Discovery Cycle

In your most innovative work, you may have to do more than one pivot in discovery, and, frankly, you may need to make even more in each of the following three phases of customer development. The world would be so much simpler if we were always right, but, to quote Monica Martinez, HSC's executive director, "It is up to us to be bold enough to take risks and do our work better and faster so that we can use our power and potential to solve big problems."

8

Validation I: Get Ready to Get Big

Thanks to the discovery phase, you've gotten this far because you understand a problem in the world and you have a solution (a value hypothesis) that works for a handful of people or cases. Validation is about using lean methodology to understand how your innovation spreads and is adopted in the field. It takes full advantage of one of the pillars of the lean startup success—the ability to measure the impact of your actions faster than ever before. Measurable, replicable results will be your watchword in this phase.

Validation is the search for a growth hypothesis with real legs. You will be running tests on most if not all of the Lean Change Canvas with the goal of testing and evolving a core growth hypothesis. The goal is a full, tested model, not of the value your innovation delivers but of how the innovation is adopted and spreads. You don't need to pioneer new ways to reach people (although in this process you might!). To innovate for growth, you need to take an experimental route (principle 2) to testing and documenting those ways.

You can think of validation as two distinct Build–Measure–Learn loops. The first is focused on how you prime the pump and "get" adoption by people, institutions, and funders—the nuts and bolts of adoption for your innovation. The second loop focuses on exploring the path that can make it big enough to be worth moving forward.

In lean startup practice, you've validated your innovation when you've achieved "product/market fit"—a match between your service or product and its intended targets that leads to widespread adoption. Validation is the way great ideas become big change.

Validation

It's one of the world's biggest problems, but nobody talks about it. That was the challenge Rachel Weidinger was faced with when she was asked to help get people to care about oceans. *The* perennial problem for oceans activists and policy-making to protect the oceans is simply that, for the vast majority of people across a planet that is 72 percent covered in seawater, oceans never come up in conversation. And it's pretty hard to preserve something that is hardly ever mentioned.

Rachel's organization is called Upwell, and it was formed based on a proven problem hypothesis—that conversations about oceans are far too rare—and a proven solution hypothesis—that increased conversation would lead to increased action. These hypotheses are core to the work of dozens of oceans advocacy organizations. Upwell's job was to figure out how to grow the oceans conversation to a scale where it could finally start to make a difference to the fate of the seas. To do that, it had to develop a replicable way to increase conversations about the ocean.

Validation is about precisely that job—taking an innovation that's proven to work (a validated *value hypothesis*) and seeing if it can be used by enough people to make a difference. You can think of the validation phase as having just two goals:

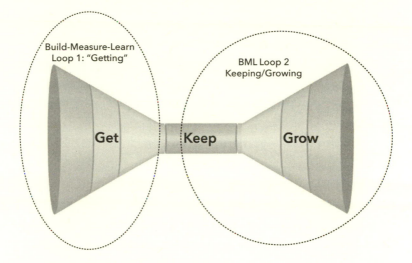

Figure 8.1 The Get-Keep-Grow Funnels

1. To understand how to "get" to your targets (what leads to their *adoption* of your innovation), and
2. To understand how to "keep and grow" the number of targets you are reaching and the depth of their adoption (what *retains and expands their adoption*).

These two components of how an innovation will grow define its *growth hypothesis*. Validation is best understood as two sequential Build–Measure–Learn loops built around these goals (see Figure 8.1). You graduate from the first loop to the second when you've got a good model for how to reach your targets. That Get model includes all that it takes (money, human and political capital, time, and other resources) to successfully deliver your innovation to relevant targets.

Before Upwell could actually influence ocean conversations, it had to understand the kinds of conversations that were already going on, who and what influenced those conversations and what sparked new ones, and timing issues, as well as what software was available to monitor conversations and how many interventions they could drive given their overall budget and staffing. (Because their funding wasn't directly driven by success with driving conversations—unlike commercial products, the oceans don't pay people to talk about them—Upwell simultaneously had to do the same process for its funder-targets.)

After you've created a replicable roadmap for getting your innovation adopted, the second loop focuses on what it takes to keep and grow your reach into your relevant targets. The Keep–Grow phase of validation seeks a replicable process for driving your innovation to larger and larger scale. Can you create a set of steps that will grow your engaged target population to the scale necessary for solving or at least satisfactorily addressing your problem?

In Upwell's case, this meant developing routines that regularly delivered results on something as fickle as online spikes in conversations about oceans, something that not a lot of people regularly discussed. It turns out that there were predictable elements to this conversation that Upwell could successfully link to over and over again to make a difference.

It takes a lot of discipline to run a good validation phase. Remember, you already know by now that your innovation solves a real problem and that there are probably some people eager to move forward quickly to solve it. Maybe even some funders are queued up. Validation is all about understanding in quantitative terms the *process* that gets you to *big* impact. It's not about testing your solution, but rather about what gets your solution out in the world and into use. So before we get into actual hypothesis testing, let's review the kinds of knowledge you are trying to generate and look at some key insights about how you'll generate them.

Priority Learning for Validation

Validation starts with a review of your Lean Change Canvas. You'll have winnowed down some of the boxes to hypotheses you've confirmed, but many will still have great but unconfirmed ideas in them. Evaluate which of the boxes are relevant to your growth hypotheses. Which ones will influence not the effectiveness of your idea but its adoption and the rate at which it will spread?

As in the discovery phase, the boxes on the righthand side will be most crucial (Targets, Relationships, Channels/Pathways). But the rest of the boxes start to be critical ingredients. What role will Partners play in augmenting your reach? Which activities and resources do you need to deploy to spread your innovation? What's the revenue and expense structure of reaching your key targets?

In the validation phase, you're going to learn a lot about three things: the *people or institutions* (targets) key to your innovation, the *motivations* that determine how they interact with your innovation, and the *timing* of interactions between people and motivations that determine how fast your innovation can grow. In validation, you're testing hypotheses about the relationships among these three things. At the end, you'll have a model that you can predictably deploy for growth.

What you want to learn about the *people/institutions* part of your innovation is whom you are targeting—specific direct targets, specific indirect targets, and/or specific funders; who influences the adoption of your innovation; and who is your most enthusiastic audience. Your primary focus should be on those enthusiasts, also known as early adopters. They are those who most want what you have to offer. Understand why by spending a lot of time with them. For example, Upwell identified a large cadre of oceans communicators who were already driving a lot of ocean conversations. Eventually, those communicators became a primary, but indirect, target for the thousands of conversations whose even broader target was the online public.

Motivations are another key learning area in the validation phase. You want to understand why people are using your service or product; how actively they will use it in terms of time, money, and/or attention; and what specific mechanisms and strategies best connect to the motivations that are moving your various targets. What are the really critical problems your innovation is solving for your targets? Get to understand these motivations as deeply as possible.

For Upwell, the original motivation was to drive conversations about marine protected areas (MPAs), a big new policy idea that has since been widely implemented. The only problem was that nobody talked about MPAs in daily chatter, ever. Out of hundreds of thousands of times the ocean was mentioned in social media, fewer than fifty references to MPAs came up every week.

Upwell did discover vibrant online conversations that engaged tens of thousands of people about the oceans that were centered on whales, sharks, and general ocean experiences, particularly in the summer when crowds started taking to beaches. These themes were the *motivations* at the core of the oceans discussion.

Finally, in validation you will learn a lot about *timing*. How long does it take for your product or service to start having an impact? What's the lifecycle of your innovation with each type of target, and, in particular, how long does it take to get each of them to engage with the change you're trying to create? In Upwell's case, within about a year of its founding it was running "minimum viable campaigns" that boosted ocean conversations on a daily basis (more on these later).

People/institutions, motivations, and timing together make up really a granular theory of growth, and the validation phase tests and hones that theory. At the end of validation, you'll have a replicable model of how these factors work together to drive growth in your innovation and the kinds of resources it takes to succeed. And you should have a good idea of how big that success can be.

Funders Are Customers, Too …

In the business world, you don't run a lot of experiments on your funders. Their job is to evaluate your ideas, your team, and your market, and either invest or not. If your growth hypothesis pans out, they will make their money back and then some.

Because the beneficiaries of innovation are often not those who pay for it, social sector entrepreneurs need to think of funders as targets as well; and to innovate in how they connect their programmatic activities back to government or philanthropic sources of revenue. Luckily, the Get–Keep–Grow funnel is perfectly adapted to testing hypotheses about funders, be they individuals reached through direct mail or groups of foundations jointly funding an initiative. The validation phase for the social sector must also be used to understand where your innovation will *get* funding, how it will *keep* it, and, ultimately, how it will *grow* funding sufficient to get to scale. This chapter focuses on validating the innovation's growth among its targets, but the analysis can be used back up the chain to develop a strong funding strategy as well.

Stay Lean!

One of the true classics of startup business literature is *Crossing the Chasm* by Geoffrey Moore.[1] One of Moore's key insights is that a major reason that new companies and new ideas fail is that the founders confuse the model of how an innovation gets big

---

1 Geoffrey A. Moore, *Crossing the Chasm: Marketing and Selling Disruptive Products to Mainstream Customers*, 3d edn. (New York: HarperCollins, 2014).

among early adopters with how it's going to play in the mainstream market. The largest source of failure lies in assuming that the entire mainstream market will be like the early adopters. In doing so, many companies overextend themselves prematurely.

Nonprofits and government face similar pressures to mistake early adopters for the early majority. The political flush of early success breeds overconfidence about the scale that will be possible in the near future. The key to crossing Moore's chasm is staying lean by focusing on the smallest possible group within the mainstream market you hope to conquer. In this way you can preserve the capital you need to experiment and pivot toward an even better solution that can eventually be adopted by the majority of voters, politicians, or other constituencies.

Here are a few insights for staying lean in the validation phase (we'll expand on these later in the chapter):

Measure the cost of hypothesis testing. If you were able, you started measuring the cost of experimentation in the discovery phase of customer development as a way to stretch your resources for driving experiments. Validation is about the rate of growth, and innovation accounting sets the metrics for affecting growth. One of the most important things you can know in the whole customer development cycle is how much it is costing you to learn what works and how quickly that learning is taking place.

As soon as possible in the validation phase, start measuring what each hypothesis test will cost and how much you learn from it. Rigorous innovation accounting has made it possible for some software companies to drive down the cost of innovation and testing to the point where they now move from testing two new versions a year to publishing dozens of new versions of their product *every day*. Imagine the possibilities for social change innovation if you can continually introduce validated improvements.

Go deep, not big. Validation can be a heady time for a new idea ("Foundation X is writing us a check!" or "Senator Y *loves* the idea!").[2] But you probably still don't really know what's going to make your innovation take off. Keep lean as your watchword through validation. Don't hire anybody new unless they're essential to this phase of hypothesis testing. Keep the leadership of the innovation hands-on and focused on the few people actually using the innovation. You want your "inventors" still in the field here, not evangelizing externally before everyone inside your team understands what's really going on.

Finally, you're going to want to be careful about how you set priorities and how you adapt the innovation based on experience and user feedback. We'll look at this in more detail in the second stage of validation.

Work backward from what you need to learn. Often when you're innovating, the people you're serving don't even know they need the thing you are trying to create. Plumbers and building owners didn't know they needed low-flow toilets in the early 1980s in New York because they weren't used to paying for water based on usage. Workers in nonunionized industries often don't imagine the value a union could bring to their quality of life and earning power. Businesspeople we were targeting with Smarter, Cleaner, Stronger had no idea that climate policy and clean energy could strengthen the business climate as well. Budget offices, committees, and philanthropic funders often can't see the ground-level dynamics that have pointed you toward making a difference.

---

2 Going deep and working backward are actually foundational to lean practice in industry from the shop floor to software coding teams. You can read much more about them in case studies across the web. Just search for "small batches" and "work-in-progress inventory" along with "lean." Or take a look at the discussion on www.leanchange.net.

Deep, Not Big: The Case for Small Batches

Almost everyone in the social sector has stuffed a lot of envelopes at some point in our careers. That activity is one of the best illustrations of the lean principle of small batches.

If you have 1,000 identical letters to get out, the first instinct is often to queue the job up with a printing station, a folding station, a stuffing station, a sealing station, and a stamping station. It turns out to be much more efficient to just do each letter, one at a time, through the whole process. Why? Because there are always unexpected glitches that can ruin big batches if that's how you start out. The paper can be the wrong size, the folds not quite right for the envelope address window, and so on. This is an experiment that's been replicated numerous times with the same outcome ... small batches beat big batches.

The small-batch principle is just another example of going deep instead of big at this phase of your innovation. The experience of driving adoption and growth, one person at a time, will be invaluable to building a truly scalable deployment model.

What this means in practice is that you want to minimize the size of modifications you make to your service or product. Focus instead on pushing out each little improvement and learning from those releases quickly. Delight your targets with continuous tweaks in their favor rather than frustrating them and your own team with the bottlenecks that big-batch approaches always introduce.

So you're not always going to be responding directly to your targets' expressed needs and wants. Your focus in validation should be instead on what you really need to learn to drive adoption of your innovation. As Eric Ries notes, "It's not the customer, but rather our hypothesis about the customer" that defines the work you need to do.[3]

---

3 Ries, *The Lean Startup*, p. 201.

Upwell's "customer," or direct target, was a group of founda-tions seeking to drive more oceans conversation. Those founda-tions were particularly concerned about getting people to discuss marine protected areas. After looking at the initial conversation data, it was clear to Upwell that it needed to test new hypotheses about both the funder-customers (as in "would foundations fund conversation building if MPAs weren't the focus?) and even the indirect targets, who were the public engaging in more general oceans conversations.

Design in feedback. From the very beginning, make sure you've incorporated ways to get signals from the people you're reach-ing. Collect data on their reactions as quickly as possible. Doing so will net you the data you need to create a continuous flow of feedback for learning. A beneficial side effect is that this effort should earn you the trust of your key targets as they learn that you are really listening for their needs.

Be ready for success. You will probably spend a lot of time in the validation phase, so remember to be patient. It's in this phase that you will prove that your innovation will be broadly adopted or not. It's here that you'll test if your innovation stands a chance of making the difference the world needs. There will be several pivots based on what you learn about your direct and indirect targets and your funders. If you don't hit a growth wall, at some point your innovation will take off. Chapter 11 will cover custom-er creation—the details of ramping up and institutionalizing your innovation. That moment is what you're striving to create in the validation phase. Be ready to recognize it, because that's when you'll need to turn on the jets.

Just because your innovation works doesn't mean it will grow, and just because it will grow doesn't mean it will grow big enough. Validation breaks out these two questions into two Build–Measure–Learn cycles. When and if you've worked your way through both of them to a confirmed growth hypothesis, you move on to the next phase, creation, where you pour significant resources into creating both value *and* growth. Meanwhile, validation is the crucial next step to understanding if you can make the difference you hope to achieve.

9

Validation II: Priming the Pump

In the discovery phase, you found that your solution was important to a fairly large number of people, and in learning that you started the process of validating the first part of your growth hypothesis. Simply put, there's a series of steps that "got" your initial targets (whether direct or indirect targets or funders) to adopt and/or to fund your solution. The first Build–Measure–Learn loop in validation is devoted to refining your minimum viable product so that you can *get adoption* by your targets over and over again.

This first loop focuses on an adoption funnel, which is wide at the beginning of engagement to represent all the people you will be reaching out to, and narrower at the end to represent all those who actually did engage with your innovation.

The work of the first loop is all about the interaction between the innovation itself and how you plan to drive its adoption. There are two components to this interaction: the marketing infrastructure for the solution (positioning, marketing materials, people, budgets, media, and other factors), and the solution itself.

Figure 9.1 The Build-Measure-Learn Cycle for "Get" Activities

Marketing Infrastructure: The Drivers of Adoption

You need to test all the key components of your marketing infrastructure in this BML loop. They include:

1. *A purpose statement.* With the MVP developed, you need language to describe it consistently both within and outside your organization. You need to craft a statement of the innovation's purpose that makes it easy for people, particularly your targets, to understand. The purpose statement should include information about who the innovation is for, what problem it solves, what type of product or service it is, what benefit it delivers, and how it is new and/or compares to alternatives.

2. *Outreach/marketing materials.* Start with what you used in developing your MVP. What resonated in your descriptions to funders, users, partners, and other targets? Boil that down into

The Positioning Statement:
The Business Equivalent of the Purpose

Steve Blank argues that the positioning statement is an essential component of the validation process for business startups. You can craft one and see if it works for your social sector innovation using this positioning template:

For [customer/target]:

- *Who wants/needs* [compelling need]
- *The* [product or service] is a [type of product or service]
- *That provides* [key benefit]
- *Unlike* [existing options/alternatives]

Here's a sample for the Smarter, Cleaner, Stronger program from chapter 4. It's focused on a statement for senators, who were indirect targets of the effort. A similar positioning statement for editorial boards (the program's direct targets) and funders can be found at www.leanchange.net/positioning.

For US senators who need an understanding of the economic benefits of climate policy, the Smarter, Cleaner, Stronger campaign is peer-reviewed research that informs your constituencies of the economic impact of climate policy, unlike existing economic research publications.

your first drafts and then start testing how effective these materials and messages are with the key audiences and targets you're seeking to engage.

3. Staff. Evaluate whether your founding team has all the skills you need to effectively drive adoption of your innovation. If the core skill is community organizing or voter mobilization and that's not your strong suit, hire someone who has done that before and knows how to do it well. If you need someone who has built large memberships for a new museum, bring them onboard. But if you can run your tests without new staff, do so. Keep your team lean. Whether you bring in new people or not, the whole team needs to be committed to finding the model that works, not to deploying an old formula in a new situation. Sometimes this makes bringing on the right people harder because, although you want them for their expertise at a particular form of outreach and engagement, you also want them engaged in experimentation that may change the way they've done things in the past. You can't guarantee to them that you'll do things the way they're used to. No matter what, stay hands-on. This is *not* the time for the initial team to start focusing more broadly. It should be all hands on deck to apply the initial focus to this critical phase.

4. *Explicit roadmaps (adoption, channels, others as necessary).*
You and your team need explicit roadmaps for the ways your innovation gets out in the world and adopted. Use the Channels/Pathways hypotheses from your Lean Change Canvas as a starting point to test the delivery channels you plan on using. Will you be directly serving the beneficiaries of your innovation or delivering it through partners or other intermediaries? Who/what lies between you and your targets, and how will your innovation travel through and with them?

For an adoption roadmap, simply write out the methods you used to get your innovation out there so far and start testing against that. Figure 9.2 shows an example from the campaign by Smarter, Cleaner, Stronger to reach editorial boards.

You may need roadmaps for the financial and social capital you need for your innovation as well. Which funders will be behind you and when? Are there different funders for different au-

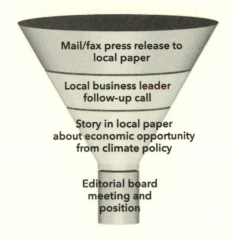

Figure 9.2 Sample Adoption Roadmap: Smarter, Cleaner, Stronger and Editorial Boards

diences and/or stages of your innovation? A power map can be an invaluable place to track your hypotheses about the political and social routes to success. Who holds power in the systems you are trying to influence, and how can you approach and influence them? (Resources for power-mapping can be found at www.lean-change.net/powermap.)

5. *Outside advisors.* There are a lot of moving pieces in your growth hypothesis and you can't be expert in all of them. Look at your roadmaps and pull in key actors for the parts of the roadmap you'd like extra help with. At a minimum, consider funders (potential and actual), subject matter experts, community members (representing those benefitting from your innovation), and representatives of some of your key political and social capital. The latter could be staff to key legislators, members of an impacted business community, or key partners. Let these advisors know that you need them to help you design and evaluate tests in how you grow your innovation to scale.

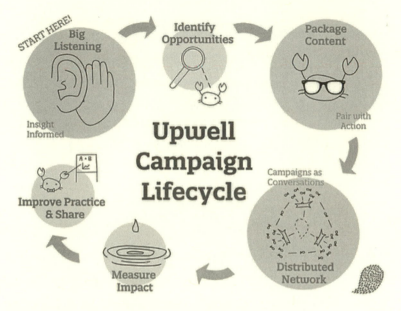

Figure 9.3 Sample Adoption Cycle for Upwell
Source: 2014 Creative Commons Attribution ShareAlike 3.0 Unported License.

6. *Metrics and dashboards.* The validation phase is all about measuring how your innovation grows, and a consistent set of evaluation metrics is a critical part of getting through successfully. You've built a solution and the tools to drive it into the world. An analytics dashboard helps you visualize these metrics and helps you learn the dynamics of adoption and, in the second BML loop, the dynamics of growth.

The priority in validation is collecting great data about the rate of learning (innovation accounting) rather than total impact, and then driving efficient experiments about how those rates create a viable business. The experiments themselves can use a number of tools to influence the rates, and there are easy-to-use tools on the Web that make implementing the experiments increasingly simple (see www.leanchange.net/growthtools).

One of the most important tools for the validation phase is *cohort analysis*. Understanding cohort effects and how to monitor them are foundational to any analysis because they give you an understanding of which hypotheses explain which outcomes at any given moment. Cohort analysis is the main tool for doing this, and it involves segmenting your results according to different categories of users. It allows you to dive below your aggregate results to understand which variable in your adoption and growth process is having which influence.

Typical cohorts chosen for analysis are based on:

- When were they engaged? (Which month, for example—the most common metric?)
- What part of the Get–Keep–Grow funnel are they in? Where in your solution do they drop off?
- What version of your solution were they using? (For example, the one from last month or the one from last year?)

A/B testing is another critical tool that has become a staple of online customer development—to present customers with two

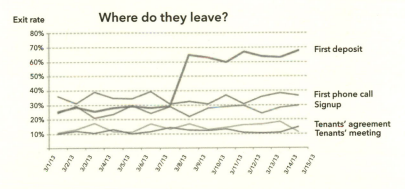

Figure 9.4 Cohort Analysis: People Who Made Their First Deposits in March Had a Much Worse Experience

(or more) different versions of either the innovation or the marketing materials and then compare the results—but it can be used in products and services in the physical world as well.

The A/B test can be as simple as sending out identical emails or flyers with different subject lines/headlines and then evaluating the outcomes, such as how many emails are opened or how many people respond to which flyer. Any binary hypothesis can be tested this way, and it's best to keep things simple and to test hypotheses sequentially. If you are so inclined and you have a large enough sample size, you can test multiple hypotheses at once, as well as interactions between elements in your innovation and/or your marketing infrastructure.

Incentives can be injected into any of your hypothesis testing to accelerate uptake. These incentives can be treated like a special

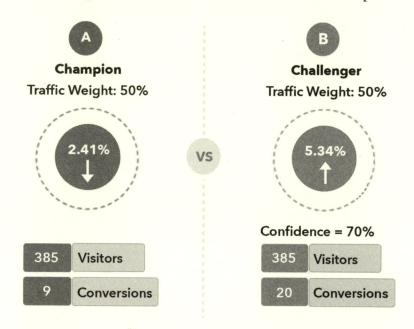

Figure 9.5 Schematic Dashboard for A/B Testing

cohort with similar tools. You can test paid growth or various virality mechanisms by giving users incentives to drive the outcomes you're seeking. Incentives can include such things as gifts, access to information, and priority status.

Customer service provides crucial data and, increasingly, its quality can be monitored and driven. You can run growth experiments based on high-touch customer service, offer personalized service via email or phone, and make feedback easy so that your users can tell you what they think and you can respond with improvements. A number of excellent combined systems both keep track of your learning and help with the customer service (you can find pointers to some of these systems at www.leanchange. net/tools/a-b).

You've built a solution and developed the tools to drive that solution into the world. Measuring and learning are the steps that come next.

Optimizing Adoption

It's time, again, to get out of the building.

This time, in addition to your innovation, you're equipped with a clear purpose statement; outreach materials; staff (not too many!); roadmaps for funding, channels/partners, and adoption; advisors; and a dashboard waiting to be filled with results of your tests for all of the above. You've developed these partially based on your success so far with those who validated your solution hypothesis in the discovery phase.

Attach performance goals to each element of the infrastructure (see Table 9.1 for samples), and start with other potential early adopters. Test components of your marketing infrastructure and rates of adoption in a very hands-on way. Sit with your prospects/targets, call people who enroll online, and ask all of them what's working and what's not, and then compile those answers.

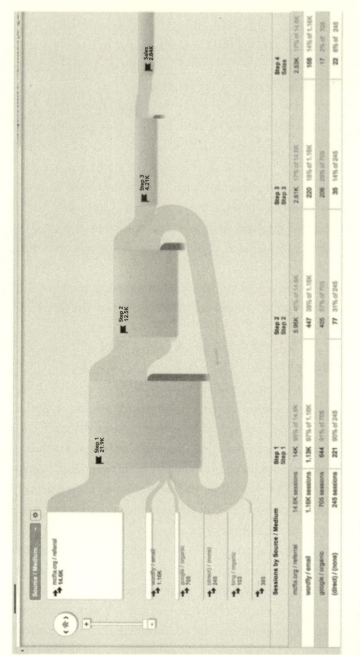

Figure 9.6 Sample Dashboard

Table 9.1 Sample Key Adoption Hypotheses/Metrics

Smarter, Cleaner, Stronger	National Museum of the American Indian	Catalog Choice	New York City Toilet Bowl Retrofit
Media outlets will pick up a story after our release 75 percent of the time	Attendance during the opening month will be 200,000	Each $100 of Google AdWords generates 10 users	$1,000 spent on recruiting plumbers nets 20 plumbers, or $50/plumber
Editorial boards will take a meeting 40 percent of the time	20% of online visitors will sign up for online membership	The click-through rate for online ads is 1.5 percent	20 percent of plumbers at orientation meeting enroll in program
Senators' staff will have noticed local media coverage 90 percent of the time	5 percent of online visitors will enroll for sponsoring membership	The open rate for email solicitation from environmental partners is 5 percent	Each plumber retrofits, on average, 50 toilet bowls/month
Local environmental funders will take a meeting 80 percent of the time		20 percent of users who get to the signup page do so	

Your goal is to validate your adoption model, every tool in your toolkit, every step on your roadmap. In this first BML loop, you don't care so much about growth as about a granular, replicable understanding of how your product or service gets adopted to begin with.

The metaphor we use to structure the validation phase is the Get–Keep–Grow funnel, and this first BML loop is limited to its first part, the "get" part of the funnel. How people become aware of your innovation and enter your funnel will depend on where in the social sector you work. The cloud at the top of Figure 9.7 lists some of the most likely ways people will first encounter your

Figure 9.7 Get Funnel for Products versus Online Acquisition

innovation. You can set targets and measure the effectiveness of each of these awareness-drivers.

The funnel may be specific to your innovation, but Figure 9.7 also illustrates how Get funnels fall into one of two general categories: innovations that are delivered in a physical channel and those delivered online. The process of engaging people for a product or service that is delivered physically, in the real world, can be understood as having four stages. (Of the four example programs discussed in chapter 4, only one is *not* physical, Catalog Choice.)

In this phase of validation, you want to understand how your marketing effort and your innovation itself contribute to moving each individual target through the funnel. Understand what drives the increasing commitment targets make as they move through awareness, interest, consideration, and, finally, adoption. In an online context (like Catalog Choice), two steps define the Get: acquiring targets and activating them.

In both contexts the job is the same: understand why people (or other targets such as funders or organizations) stay in the funnel or drop out. Is there something about how you're marketing the innovation that stops them from adopting it? To find out, follow up with those who don't adopt more than with those who do, and don't hesitate to call people, even if you've been acquiring them online. Start with the places where there's the most attrition and look for patterns either in how you're reaching your targets or in the product or service itself. Then adjust your innovation and your marketing to reduce the rate of dropoff in your funnel.

This first Build–Measure–Learn loop focuses *both* on your innovation and on the marketing infrastructure you've chosen to disseminate it. The trickiest part of validation is managing this interaction. On the one hand, there's the temptation to simply separate the two. It would be nice if the path to change were as simple as hiring a staff, putting together marketing collateral and a plan, and pushing your idea out into the world. But the most successful innovations are those that embed the seeds of their adoption and growth *within the solution itself.*

The software world is replete with examples of this interaction. Think of how joining Facebook immediately starts you adding even more people to that network. Union organizing is a classic example of the importance of this interaction in the social sector. The product at hand is a new union local in a new workplace, and every time union organizers choose a new sector to organize, they're innovating, finding ways to empower workers in a new political, social, and workplace environment. They need to develop a marketing infrastructure, a set of replicable tools they use to approach individual workers and to put pressure on employers and political leaders, and other methods to keep people in the funnel. But the good organizer's most important tool is the way in which the workers themselves define and disseminate the task of organizing. How are workers' goals and interactions designed into the "product," in this case a new union? How can the union be designed to maximally satisfy those goals? An organizer who accomplishes that will build a more powerful local with more members who join faster; and a new generation of labor organizers have started using lean startup–like tools to expand into new worker populations and to challenge traditional organizing models.

The critical part of validation isn't the problem or the solution (as it was in the development phase) but how *growth* is embedded in the product or service, how the innovation is designed to prime its own pump. The Get part of the funnel is the entry point for managing this process. The next part of validation focuses on the second key dimension of growth—how, once you have an engaged set of targets, you keep them using your innovation and growing their numbers by making them agents of their own scaling.

10

Validation III:
Keep + Grow = Scale

Keep and Grow: Can Your Innovation Get Big Enough?

The Get phase of validation is where you learn how to reliably turn prospective users of your innovation into actual users. When you've got that down in the form of roadmaps, you can start running a Build–Measure–Learn loop around the things they do *as users* that keep them using the innovation and generate growth by spreading the innovation to other users. Keeping and growing are the key lessons of the second loop (see Figure 10.1).

Keep

You've already engaged some people using your product or service. Now is the time to find out what's keeping them there and how you can make that even better. There are a number of strategies for doing this that you can put through your BML loop:

1. *Call on your users.* You've already interacted with them significantly as part of discovery. Call these early users regularly (alternatively, be in close contact with them via email), and you can even go so far as to form an advisory group of these early users to keep your finger on the pulse of your "customers." These calls

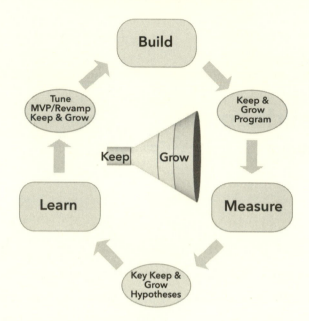

Figure 10.1 The Keep–Grow Loop

should come from the founding team, the people with the original vision who are able to hear directly how it needs to evolve.

2. Measure your users' engagement and satisfaction. You can go to town developing metrics for key parts of your solution and then finding out which parts really make users happy and which don't. You especially want to understand why someone is abandoning your innovation. What part of your solution is failing them, causing users to abandon it?

3. Experiment actively with how to get your users and/or organizations to "stick." Are there additional activities or offerings that would increase the rate at which people stick with the innovation? Can you create rewards or perks for longevity? Can you send them additional information that further engages them and keeps them onboard?

4. *Put your engagement "experts" on those you are losing.* Try to put your best foot forward so that you can see how much of disengagement is self-motivated versus something wrong with your product or service.

In the private sector, these "keep" efforts can be focused predominantly on customers. In the social sector, you will need to focus on keeping a number of different types of targets engaged. Each of the steps to keep users should be thought about separately for direct targets, indirect targets, and funders. But the good news is that rigorous thinking and measurement on these issues will earn you the respect of your funders and colleagues and make it easier to fund-raise and sustain the political and social capital that underpins your innovation.

Grow

At the end of the day, you're innovating to solve a problem, and a natural question at any stage of this process is whether you will make a big enough dent in the problem to be worth it. How big do you need to be to make a difference? To stay adequately funded by philanthropic and/or government sources? Was your initial goal to make a dent in the problem, or to solve it once and for all? Such questions can help you define success for the overall validation phase.

You now understand how you get and keep customers and how you engage your users or drive attrition. You can now build on that data and turn to the best thing you can get from those you seek to serve—growth.

The Sources of Growth

In the social sector, there are two main sources of growth. The first is to deliver more value to the people you're targeting. You can do this by having your innovation encompass more and more of your issue area and your targets' interests by deepening your service to them and by broadening your impact and your adoption with them. In the private sector, these strategies have names like "unbundling," "cross-selling," and "upselling," and are all about increasing the dollars/customer ratio. In the social sector, that ratio can be understood as impact/target.

Table 10.1 How Big Is Big Enough? Meaningful Goals for Lean Startups in the Social Sector

Smarter, Cleaner, Stronger	National Museum of the American Indian	Catalog Choice	New York City Toilet Bowl Retrofit
The most important media outlet in 8 out of 17 target states endorses climate policy for economic reasons (we needed four votes in the US Senate) Raise funding of $25,000/state	Attendance will grow to 400,000/month Revenue from membership will cover 30 percent of operating expenses	Save 1 million trees by reducing junk mail Reach 1 million consumers Get to "break-even" financially – independent of philanthropy	Replace 1.5 million toilet bowls Save 100 million gallons of water per day

The second source of growth is simply to reach more targets, be they individuals, institutions, or funders. This second form of growth is focused purely on increasing the raw numbers going through your funnel (see Figure 10.2).

Give Them More!

One of the main ways to grow your impact is to modify your innovation in ways that deepen your engagement with your targets. Let's use the example of New York City's Toilet Bowl Ret-

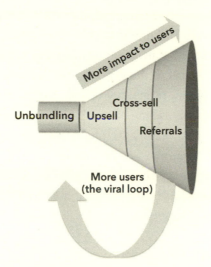

Figure 10.2 The Two Dimensions of the "Grow" Funnel

rofit program to understand the three key ways you can deepen engagement. Once the New York City water agency had established that we could get toilet bowls switched out, we expanded the activities we were asking plumbers to do. Soon they were not only replacing toilets but also showerheads and faucets. We were able to exploit the fact that we were already in the household to drive more water-conserving "product" into that environment and achieve greater impact. In the private sector, this is called cross-selling. Thinking about ways to get more impact out of the same population is the social sector's equivalent.

A second way to deepen engagement is to increase the amount of a specific product or service you deliver to each target. In the toilet program, we eventually mandated that any building owner participating in the program retrofit at least 70 percent of the toilets in a building, ensuring that we weren't frittering dollars on one-off installations and instead maximizing our impact and reach in every location.

A third way to deepen engagement is to unbundle elements of the original innovation into separate solutions. We didn't do that very much in the toilet program, but a good example of this might be a health and wellness program that originally offered a one-stop shop where targets exercised and received counseling and diet tips. An unbundling of the program might involve sending customers to a gym and then having separate meetings with a nutritionist and a counselor. Unbundling can help deepen your impact with targets by deepening the offering itself. It can also increase revenue and/or fundraising by providing more touch points for funders' support.

Find More of Them ...

Cross-selling, upselling, and unbundling are all standard practices to drive growth and deepen relationships with your targets by expanding your solution. The second major approach to growth involves simply increasing the raw numbers of people your innovation is reaching.

Here's the bottom line to the lean startup approach to expanding the number of targets you serve: *it's all about the rates and not about the totals.* Far too often, we get excited about the total number of people we're serving or some other absolute metric of total impact. For an innovation to have truly massive impact, the important thing is to focus on understanding what drives the rates of growth rather than the total impact.

Rates have always been the important variable for growth, but lean startups are able to focus on them more directly because our ability to understand and to measure these rates has grown exponentially over the last decade. Three archetypal rate examples:

1. *Churn.* Say you've found a source of 20,000 new signups or members per month. If your churn is 5 percent, you are also los-

ing 5 percent of your members per month. When your membership reaches 400,000 people after about two years, your growth
will stop because you'll be losing as many members as you gain
each month.

You can achieve huge growth simply by focusing on serving
your targets so well that they never leave. If your targets never leave (or, more realistically, leave more slowly than the rate
at which new targets engage), you will grow. The relevant rate
to this kind of growth is simply the ratio of new targets to lost
targets, and it works like compound interest. The lower your attrition (or churn), the higher your rate of growth. This approach
can work as a way to think about funders as well, particularly
if you raise money from individual donors. The Build-Measure-
Learn loop's goal is to maximize the compounding rate by understanding what drives down attrition while maintaining your
ability to get new targets.

2. Virality. Another major form of growth can come from the
way your targets themselves spread your innovation, product, or
service. Growth driven by targets falls under the catch-all category of "viral growth." This is the business Upwell is in with every
Minimum Viable Campaign, and their viral component comes
from having content that users themselves share with others to
experience rapid dissemination of that content and an explosion
in the number of conversations about the ocean.

Upwell uses the power of social media's inherent sharing
mechanisms to grow its impact, but a product or service can "go
viral" simply by being so excellent that users share it with one another in large numbers. Viral growth has the advantage of costing nothing but the expense of designing in a viral feature. True
virality is measured by the virality coefficient, which is simply the
number of new users generated by an average existing user.

3. Paid acquisition. When the value of new users significantly exceeds the cost of getting them, then you can drive growth simply by paying for it. The Toilet Bowl Retrofit program was an example of this. Because reduced water flow reduced demands on expensive infrastructure like sewage treatment plants, the program saved New York City money with every toilet bowl installed. The city therefore was willing to pay to grow the user base for the program.

The relevant rate to optimize in the Build–Measure–Learn loop is the differential between the cost of acquiring a new user and the benefits or net savings of having served that user. In the social sector, a vital issue is also that the costs and benefits often do not accrue to the same organization, but creative programs can use creative finance to connect the dots and drive a compelling innovation.

Staying Lean ...

Validation is an exciting process because you are testing the possibilities for truly massive growth. At the same time, you can be overwhelmed by the number of possible changes to your innovation and the permutations on how you reach your targets. At the end of the day, though, there are only two ways to truly grow your innovation:

1. Get more people to use it.
2. Get people to use it more.

Focus your experiments and your work to tweak your innovation and your marketing on these two mechanisms to keep the validation phase focused and on target. Any additional modifications or improvements you are considering at this stage can be pushed back until after you've gotten through validation. Your goal now is simply to test growth hypotheses until you're sure you've figured it out.

Product/Market Fit: The End of Validation

The validation phase has been about testing the key ingredients to growth: how you get users, and how you keep them and get more of them. The learning for the first should have resulted in a replicable roadmap for driving new users to your product or service. The learning for the second should have resulted in a clear understanding of the rates relevant to growing your innovation and the biggest influences over those rates.

You've been running experiments that reshaped your product or service (to drive getting, keeping, and growing users), you've tested your marketing materials and infrastructure, and you've tried a few different approaches to expanding your reach. You've honed a dashboard to monitor the critical tests, and each of those tests should have led to an incremental pivot, taking you closer to an optimized product or service and a higher growth rate.

So when is validation over? Remember what Steve Blank told me back in 2008? "You want to build something that barely works, but if you took it away from people, they'd beg to pay you for it." You've experimented your way to this point in the validation phase, pivoting as you went to make a product and a marketing infrastructure that meets this criterion.

Marc Andreesen, one of the inventors of the first Web browser, coined the term "product/market fit" for when an innovation has undeniably crossed the chasm and is starting to be pulled into the mainstream market. In the private sector, there is a "you'll know it when you see it" view of this moment—it's when the floodgates open and you can't seem to meet demand fast enough and the revenue from demand promises to be enough to generate real growth.

The main difference for product/market fit in the social sector is that most social sector innovations don't generate a profit. The signal of success may never mean that you're turning a profit, bringing in more money than you're spending. So product/market fit for social innovation has instead to meet two, and perhaps even three, standards of success.

First, the innovation must work at getting, keeping, and growing users and impact. There needs to be a replicable and scalable model for delivering the innovation. Second, there needs to be a sustainable funding model. Social innovations do not preclude a revenue stream derived from sales, but more often they are dependent on grants or contracts from government and/or charitable sources including foundations and individuals.

Product/market fit is more complex to determine for social innovations precisely because such innovation takes place in a context that is not just financial, but also involves significant social and political capital arrayed both for and against action. Innovations in health care insurance, for example, may save lives but also operate in the context of a broader debate over the appropriate role and scale of government.

The case of Upwell suggests a third, potentially critical dimension of product/market fit. Despite proven success at driving new conversations and traffic, Upwell's model failed to get product/market fit with its funders, who, at the end of the day, had hoped to see conversations about their specific concerns (marine protected areas) driven up. Upwell generated a tremendous amount of validated learning, but that lesson—that collaborative messaging by the oceans community could expand the public's engagement with oceans issues—flew in the face of a fiercely competitive ecosystem of oceans advocacy organizations. That community was simply not ready to build the conversation together—for example, by tweeting each other's success stories or pointing to each other's Web resources during peak traffic opportunities.

So social sector product/market fit must also take into account this social and political context. At a first order, consider the risks posed by opportunity costs (as discussed in chapter 3). Even if an innovative solution has reached product/market fit from a number of objective criteria, does it do so at a rate sufficient to justify providing it with external funding compared to other potential innovations? Any successful innovation has to meet the threshold not just of good growth, but of growth big enough to make the kind of difference the innovator and/or her investors think is important.

Before you proceed to institutionalize your innovation, it's worth undertaking an evaluation of the *negative* political and social capital arrayed against it. In the private sector, innovations have to have a model of sustainable competitive advantage—that is, the ways in which they will thrive in the face of anticipated competition. Similarly, social innovations need to account for the political and social headwinds their innovation may face. Put another way, your beneficiaries may love your solution, but your funders, regulators, or other members of the public may hate it. Evaluate your product/market fit then in terms not just of your beneficiaries and funders, but also of the broader environment in which you'll be operating.

Validation is over when you've considered all of these concerns with the lean startup methodology. If you know the specific mechanisms that get, keep, and grow your impact; how to predictably drive those mechanisms; and whether the impact is significant enough to justify the time, money, and energy you have to put in to get it, then you're ready to move forward.

Now it's time to launch and to build an organization to bring your innovation to scale.

11

Creation:
Scaling Impact

Congratulations! Now it's time to create something! You and your colleagues have worked hard to get to this point. You know that your innovation works for real people in the real world, and you have a decent idea of how to get, keep, and grow those you most clearly want to target. Now's the time to make big impact by building the right organization to scale your innovation or by changing the organization that's incubated your innovation to make an even bigger impact.

Steve Blank, the father of the lean startup movement, argues that startup companies aren't really businesses, they're organizations in search of a profit model. (You are, after all, not really a business unless you're making a profit.) And he recommends delaying any decisions about how to scale and/or institutionalize delivery of your innovation until you're pretty sure about your profit model.

This means, first and foremost, that you keep the innovators/inventors themselves as close to customers as possible, getting firsthand data from them. You also delay any hiring that assumes a particular delivery model until you've reached product/market fit and your innovation starts flying off the shelves. In business, this translates as the fewest sales and marketing people possible until you know exactly how you're going to sell and market your innovation based on the validation phase.

Ideally, the same holds true for social sector innovations. Up until this point, you've been testing whether your innovation delivers a real solution and whether you can get customers (or targets) to adopt it in a repeatable way. In the creation phase of customer development, you'll start testing hypotheses about how to scale the operation of your innovation—basically, how to reach a lot of people and then how to institutionalize an organization optimized to keep expanding your impact.

The idea is to presume as little as possible about what structure will be optimal for delivering your product or service until you've run the experiments to show that you can deliver value. A great side benefit is that until now you've kept hiring and other expenses to a minimum, preserving capital for the learning you need to do about the structure of your innovation before you can really focus on growth.

At this point, businesses are usually built with only one real bottom line in mind—maximizing profit. Social sector startups have far more variables to optimize. Some do, in fact, need to make more money than they spend (the most basic definition of "profit") because they don't have other options for funding. Most supplement the income they generate from services, memberships, fees, grants, or contracts. Many (like churches and think-tanks) collect a negligible amount of income from anywhere and rely almost entirely on charitable giving from individuals and foundations. Social sector organizations often deliver far more value, even financially, than they cost, but the hallmark of our sector is that the benefits accrue more broadly than the expenses. The people paying for them are thus different from the beneficiaries (see chapter 3 for more on this key distinction).

Scale in the social sector is therefore achieved in more diverse ways than the private sector, and it's harder to boil down a prescription to a basic set of instructions. (In businesses, for example, you always have someone in charge of sales, no matter how sales happens in that particular organization.) There are nevertheless broad patterns that can help you as an entrepreneur choose organizational models for moving forward, and this chapter will help you find and shape the hypotheses that will be key to the creation of an organization and the institutionalization of your innovation.

Creation

In the customer development framework at the heart of the lean startup, the creation phase is about understanding the type of organization you need to develop to create outcomes and the branding, positioning, messaging, metrics, and type of execution that need to be at its core. Because the key innovation of lean is hypothesis testing and agile learning, it's no wonder that, as you step up in scale from your specific innovation, you will continue to test and ask questions about the very nature of the organization you are now developing. At the end of this phase, like the previous two phases, you will have a pivot-or-proceed decision to make.

Organization Functions and Positions

In the creation phase, you take a step back from your specific innovation and place it in broader context. You want to look for organizational models appropriate to the type of solution you've developed, and you can look for types along two different lines, *functional* and *positional*.

Nonprofit and government agencies drive change in one (or a combination) of the following three *functional* ways:

Function 1: Change norms and behaviors. When Santa Cruz's Homeless Services Center set about radically increasing housing placement for the homeless, it focused on changing the ways different actors in the system worked. HSC's work is an example of how many social sector innovations seek simply to shift people's attitudes and behaviors. Examples include antismoking campaigns, campaigns targeting markets (for example, to get consumers to boycott a particular product or company), new religious initiatives, or efforts to increase pet adoption. No formal laws or rules are passed, but the innovations drive change through new behaviors and/or new social expectations.

Function 2: Change laws and policies. The Smarter, Cleaner, Stronger campaign was an effort to get a majority of the US Senate to vote for climate action. Although the campaign aimed to shift business thinking on climate and clean energy, its goal was a change in US law. Rather than influencing behavior, campaigns to change laws and policies seek to bring the rule of law to bear, setting new boundaries and parameters for social and economic behavior or influencing existing institutions to act in new ways. Examples include antismoking laws, ballot initiatives or lawsuits for gay marriage, electoral campaigns (which seek to change the implementors of laws), and innovations in funding and budgeting in the public sector.

Function 3: Build social and physical products, services, and/or institutions. Worldreader focused on creating a new way of delivering literacy. While some of its innovation was in norms and behaviors, most of it was in building new social and technological pathways to get books to kids in poor countries. In each geography, they build new social institutions, sometimes with a physical manifestation (a library, a classroom, Kindle e-readers).

Worldreader is an example of the third functional approach. Other examples include hospitals, museums, and new membership organizations—basically, any innovation that results in a tangible, organized product through which people and resources flow.

Your innovation can also be distinguished by the *position* it occupies in the social landscape. This positioning is analogous to "market types" that help to narrow business strategy in for-profit startups. In the social sector, your position is defined by the relative position of your innovation or solution with respect to existing social interventions. Kristen Grimm outlines three "positions" your innovation can take, and these parallel the market types used in for-profit lean startup development. These market types are listed after the social sector name in parentheses and are useful because some social sector innovations are directly analogous to private sector counterparts:

Position 1: Fortify/amplify (existing market). A fortifying/amplifying position means your innovation is entering a conversation or activity already in progress. In the private sector, you are joining an existing market and competing against known players to sell something similar to what is already there. Overall your innovation fits well with concepts well understood by the public or your particular targets/customers. You succeed or fail based on execution in this position: your ability to grow your impact in something that is already successfully happening in the world. Additional examples of this position include new institutions (like hospitals or museums), where you are capitalizing on demand for a well-understood service (healthcare or knowledge), or when you are entering new geographies for a preexisting product or service (like a Girl Scout troop or a new library for an underserved neighborhood). You can take advantage of not being "new" to execute in a way that draws from existing hypotheses and implementation wisdom.

Position 2: Frame (new market). Your organizational positioning here is to create something entirely new, a new way of thinking, a new way of regulating, a new institution. This is the rarest of positions, so really test your assumptions. Also, since there is no precedent for the innovation, husband your resources since finding exactly the right structure may take some time.

Table 11.1 Examples of Different Starting Social Sector Positions

Position	Example
Fortify and Amplify	Smart Growth was an example of building on an existing position in favor of good urban development. By adding the word "smart" to the growth debate, environmental advocates were able to co-opt the discussion and amplify their perspective.
Frame	The book *Bowling Alone* created a new conversation about social engagement, positing the increasing isolation of individuals in American life.
Reframe	"People kill people" was a reframe of campaigns aimed at reducing gun ownership. "Guns kill people" had been ineffective. The reframe allowed the campaigns to tap into Americans' strong sense of individual responsibility as an argument against gun ownership.

Source: Based on Kristen Grimm's work; see www.spitfirestrategies.com.

Position 3: Reframe (resegmenting an existing market). Some innovations seek to redefine a problem and its existing solutions. In that case, your positioning and your organization will focus on shifting customers away from an existing way of seeing the world to a new way—your new frame. Depending on the issue and the space, this shift can be hard to achieve, but if you've done the discovery and validation phases, you're well ahead of the curve. Your work in that case should be mostly about faithfully executing the lessons you learned in the last phase. Environmentalists often engage in reframing: redefining routine activities, like driving, as wasteful and bad for the environment. It's hard!

Choose an Organization Type

In the real world, you may find yourself building hybrid organizations, mixed combinations of these functions and positions. As you launch, you need to determine how your customers, the people you will be serving and targeting, will see you. Identify a type for your organization, an initial combination of function and position from each of the three we've listed.

Like everything in customer development, you will be testing this choice. As you determine a type, it's important to continue to be clear about what you're trying to learn. The particular combination of functional and positional type you choose is critical because it represents, beyond the specific innovation you've developed, the experience that your customers will have of your organization.

Consider Catalog Choice, for example. Its offering was a new solution for a problem that didn't have a solution before: too much junk mail. This was a classic "frame" position—a completely new service to solve a problem that didn't have an existing solution. Before customers would subscribe to this new service, Catalog Choice had to define the problem to customers so they would join. Its key positioning was not around how different it was but rather its mission to save paper and the environment in a new way. It was functionally building a service.

Santa Cruz's Homeless Services Center did the hardest thing—

it sought to reframe the problem of homelessness and then to change norms and behaviors around how it was being dealt with. HSC had started by hoping to "fortify and amplify" existing approaches to homelessness. This positional type involved convincing stakeholders that they were still part of the existing establishment (hence credible) but changing things a bit to optimize the outcomes. This approach didn't work, and HSC pivoted instead to reframing the problem as one of timing—how quickly housing vouchers were converted into actual placements. To accomplish this reframing HSC had to type itself not as a team player and coordinator, but as radically different. HSC became a time-keeper—carefully tracking the "expiration date" on vouchers and shortening the time it took to put these vouchers to use. From a function perspective, HSC's work lay somewhere between a new service (Function 3) and the creation of new norms (Function 1) around the voucher system.

As you develop your organizational type, you are testing not so much your solution as the packaging and delivery of that solution. Attached to that packaging are a set of messages and metrics appropriate to a full-fledged launch of your innovation.

Messaging

Messaging is the activity that connects your type choices to your audiences, and it is of course dependent on what type you've chosen. It involves messages, messengers, and media choices (newspapers, television, radio, social media). If your product is entirely new, it's unlikely to appeal to your entire target population at the outset. You therefore choose your messages and messengers to reach early adopters who will later evangelize more broadly.

HSC, as it pivoted to a reframing position, had to radically narrow its messaging to focus on the people in the system who controlled the speed with which vouchers could get used. All of

HSC's other partners and programs became irrelevant in the face of the "one metric that matters" that HSC drove to great results.

What if your product or service is in the "fortify and amplify" position? Simple—let 'em have it! The National Museum of the American Indian was new, but it was something everybody understood—a museum and research institution. Once built, the organization's job was not to aim for small population segments, but rather to reach as broad a population as possible with a simple message: "There's a new museum in town—come visit!"

Opposition Messaging

Competition in the social sector is real, and the most serious type is from those opposed to your goals. Social sector messaging needs to take the possibility of opposition explicitly into account—there are people out there who actively disagree with what you want to do. A tool for testing your positioning with respect to this opposition is Spitfire Strategies' Opposition Message Box.

As you develop your position, fill out the box in Figure 11.1 with information on how you know those who oppose your innovation will react. The box is a tool you can use to test hypotheses about your position. After you've filled it in, keep iterating the messages within it until the "You on You" position is clearly dominant, not just in your own mind, but in a tested way with targets.

Metrics and Execution

Based on your organization type and messaging, the final stage of the creation phase is to start executing toward some goals you set for your organizational launch. These goals need to be expressed as metrics that you're striving to achieve and treated as experiments in their own right that measure whether the organization you are building is up to delivering your innovation at scale.

Figure 11.1 The Opposition Box

Them on Them	Them on You
(What the opposition says about its position)	*(What the opposition says about your innovation)*
You on Them	**You on You**
(What you say about the opposition)	*(What you say about your position)*

Your original hypothesis about your organization type remains critical here and gets further tested through how you execute on your innovation at the organizational level. From a *framing position*, your metrics will be about teaching people about a new idea, product, or service and getting some of those you hypothesize as early adopters to jump onboard.

From a *reframing position*, you need to educate targets about how your new way of approaching an old problem is better. You need to measure the speed at which they are adopting the new frame and opting into your new solution from the old one. Finally, if you are fortifying and amplifying an existing frame, you will be measuring how much traction you get overall with your innovation. Does your new approach move more people into new behaviors, institutions, or support for the new laws and policies than do the more traditional approaches that are already used in the social sector? If not, it may be time for an organizational pivot ...

Paying for It: Expenses and Income in the Creation Phase

Do you have enough money to develop the organization and to grow it? This is a key execution metric beyond the performance of your new organization and its positioning and messaging. As a startup to this point, you may have raised some money to test your hypotheses, your team may be working within a larger government or nonprofit organization, or you may be bootstrapping off the work of volunteers and your own sweat equity. In the creation phase you need to start closely monitoring expenses and revenue because they are part of the overall design of your innovation.

Expenses are a key metric, and you should align this metric to your innovation. How much does it cost to get, to keep, and to grow your targets? Ideally you can express these expenses in pipeline or funnel form, understanding how much each stage of engagement costs and what the returns are to each encounter with your target populations. If you advertise, for example, how many people does each ad bring in, and at what cost? If you're canvassing neighborhoods, what are you paying your canvassers and how many people can each canvasser reach?

At this early stage, you may still be heavily dependent on grants or government contracts to cover expenses, and you need to treat the funding sources as part of the creation phase as well. What is your positioning with respect to the funder or donors? Are you doing more of something they already understand (fortifying and amplifying), or are you creating something completely new (framing)? What is your messaging to them, and what numbers/metrics do you need to hit to keep money flowing in the door?

Most important, try to be transparent with your funders. They may not be used to it, but the lean startup approach offers real transparency about why you're innovating the way you are.

It also offers them the most bang for the buck, since you have, so far, avoided building an organization that is too big or not suited to the outcomes you are seeking. Rather, lean startup methodology has kept you efficient and focused on maximizing your desired impact.

Remember that your hypotheses rarely survive first contact with actual people. As you've pivoted to this point, you will be stretching your funders as well, whether government agencies or private foundations and individuals. As you move through the creation phase, you will have to gauge how much of the lean voyage you can bring them along for, and how many pivots your funders can stomach before getting uncomfortable.

Your positioning in relation to funders may therefore have to be different from your positioning toward your innovation's targets. You may have to cast your innovation as completely new to keep them interested, even if it's a "fortify and amplify" effort. For your functional positioning, you may be aiming to change people's behavior but have to discuss a longer-term goal of legislative reform to keep funders engaged.

As you start to scale your innovation, its funding becomes a critical part of the lean, Build–Measure–Learn cycle. At this point, you really start to measure your innovation and to develop hypotheses that are multisided—some focused on your targets and others focused on your funders, especially if they are different (and what defines the social sector is this difference).

Pivot or Exit

It's finally time for your last pivot. Until now, you pivoted based on results with customers who tried your innovation: you pivoted based on what was effective for your way to get customers, keep them, and grow their numbers. In creation, you've strung those learnings end to end and packaged them as a unified strategy in a nascent organization. The question now is this: Does it get you where you want to go?

The social sector isn't as simple as the for-profit world. There the metric is simply whether you are making a profit large enough to justify the investment. In nonprofits and government, we are expected not to make money but to solve problems. And the competition doesn't happen in a marketplace either—it takes the form of other people and organizations sometimes explicitly working against your goals. As you work through the creation phase you will start to get a sense of how big your innovation can actually get, including the answers to these questions:

- How many people can you reach, at what cost?
- How much funding can you attract to your innovation?
- Are you consistently winning against the opposition?
- How much political capital is required to keep going and to keep growing?

This is the last pivot because, if the answer is not satisfactory, then it's time to close up shop. Remember, to have gotten this far you know you have a good solution and you're able to engage targets effectively. You definitely created something of value, but nevertheless your innovation may simply not be sustainable financially or politically. Even harder, it may be doing a lot of good, but at a scale that you or your supporters don't think is big enough to justify the effort or funding. The creation phase provides a rigorous process to help you decide to stop when necessary.

On the other hand, if the answer to these questions is satisfactory to your team and to other important stakeholders, you're ready to start institutionalizing your innovation. Institutionalization is the last phase, and it's all about creating an organization to embody and grow your innovation.

12

Institutionalization: Building the Lean Organization

The fastest-growing nonprofit I ever served actually grew too fast. Big Think started with a small fellowship to Bill, its founder and one of the greatest social innovators I have ever known.[1] His idea was to change the way Americans thought about the future, to redirect our national energy toward more positive outcomes. Within a year, he had written a concept paper, recruited some incredible senior researchers, raised several hundred thousand dollars from a handful of individual donors, and scored the cover article of a national magazine.

The one metric that mattered was common for think-tanks—getting mentioned in the press. And by any measure, Big Think was swinging way above its weight class.

Within two years its budget had grown to over $2 million a year, collected from a small group of very big donors and a growing set of national foundations. Big Think had some of the country's most innovative thinkers and a superb writer/director of publications who regularly landed major articles in national magazines.

---

1 I have changed the names in this account to protect the organization and staff members' reputations.

Bill had a great instinct for media and an even greater one for donors. He had identified a solution—big new ideas for our country disseminated in mainstream news publications—and he had a pitch that foundation boards and wealthy individuals found compelling. He had a solution hypothesis that resonated with two critical targets: the mainstream media and wealthy individuals.

Toward the end of our second year in business, I had flown out for what I thought would be a routine board meeting. We arrived and the chair immediately convened an executive session to let us know that there was basically a staff revolt underway—unless we fired Bill, the staff would all resign. We all looked at each other and started wondering what had happened.

Building a Lasting, Lean Organization

The rise of Big Think was actually a wonderful case study in the first three stages of customer development. Through extensive discussions with donors (his most important target) and journalists, Bill had done discovery and found a solution for a problem that a lot of people had—a new think-tank focused on generating innovative ideas and pushing them into mainstream media. He had validated that solution by achieving astonishing success at placing stories and at getting, keeping, and growing media attention. He'd been able to create real demand for the model and to replicate and expand on the initial success.

The only problem was where to stop. The question even Bill's most ardent supporters were asking was "What does Big Think *not* do?" Having created an innovative solution for generating new ideas, Big Think, under Bill's ambitious leadership, was expanding beyond its think-tank role. Rather than turning his attention to institutionalizing this solution, Bill continued to propose new spheres of activity, like political organizing and lobbying, that left the core staff and some of the initial donors with serious doubts about Big Think's ability to execute on its original innovative mission.

The Organizational Evolution of Innovation

For the first two years, Big Think had been searching for a sustainable business model—and it had found one. At that stage, a different type of innovation is required, the innovation to build an institution that can focus and deliver the solution at as large a scale as possible.

Steve Blank points out that a successful innovation goes through three phases on its way to deployment as a mature and large-scale solution (see Figure 12.1). Most of this book has been focused on the first phase—*development*, the experimental process of discovery, validation, and creation covered in chapters 4 through 11. At the other extreme, once an innovation is scaled and fully deployed within a large institution the core energy is focused on creating replicable *processes* to reliably deliver the solution.

The end of the creation phase is the time to scale and build an organization around your innovation. You've proven it solves a problem and you know how to get, keep, and grow the people and institutions that use it. What's left is to move from rolling out a series of experiments to rolling out an organization to deliver your innovation to the world and to grow it to have the biggest impact possible.

The focus of the institutionalization phase is to codify the wisdom and direction from the development phase into a *mission* that embodies the endpoints you now understand while leaving room for innovation in how to reach them. This process holds for organizations that start from scratch as well as for innovations incubated and retained within existing organizations. Whether you're standing on your own or scaling up within another, big-

Figure 12.1 Organizational Phases

ger organization, when you complete this phase, you won't be a startup anymore.

For social sector innovation to have vast impact, the institutionalization of that innovation has to focus on four critical activities:

1. Growing the base of targets (direct, indirect, and funding) so that your impact can grow *and* be financially viable at scale.
2. Building an organization and management structure appropriate to your mission.
3. Hiring the right people for the right jobs.
4. Creating a lasting culture of innovation.

Growing the Base: From Early Adopters to the Mainstream

How you will grow your impact depends a great deal on the organization type you determined in the creation phase. Figure 12.2 revisits Moore's famous chasm diagram with three key positions superimposed. If your innovation needs to introduce a completely new frame to a new population, you shouldn't build an organization geared to a lot of people yet. Most of the work will be around reaching early adopters and converting them to your new frame.

On the other hand, if your innovation fortifies and amplifies an existing solution that is well understood by your target populations (for example, doing a better job of making consumers aware of the environmental impact of shopping), then you're in the linear part of the growth curve (Moore's Early Majority). You *can* focus on quantity over quality, pushing your solution into more and more of the mainstream set of adopters on the righthand side of the curve.

Big Think had been a classic framing innovation and had achieved astonishing momentum among visionary donors, journalists, and citizens. The challenge Bill started to face was how to set up for long-term scale. After all, if the idea was to get new ideas into American politics it wasn't enough to simply have ear-

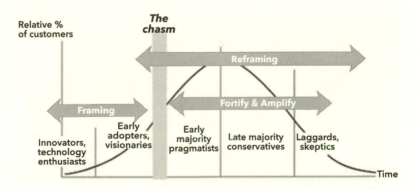

Figure 12. 2 The Chasm and Organizational Strategy/Position

ly adopters like these ideas. They had to eventually cross over to something like a majority of voters or at least policy-makers.

The complaint voiced by staff was that Bill was trying to be all things to all people. As one person put it, "We don't know what we are *not!*" Bill kept promising a broader set of innovations to a broader set of donors, terrifying staff about how they could be expected to deliver on such a wide array of expectations.

Bill committed the classic error of early success—he assumed that he could continue to grow the way he had in the early stages of the organization. Instead of evolving strategies to reach an early majority, he continued to pump out visionary ideas that excited his early adopters. Since they "got" things quickly, they also potentially got bored quickly unless he renewed their interest with another bright, shiny object.

In fact, there are two classic ways to cross the chasm, and Big Think hadn't planned for either one. The first (and most popular) is to focus all your resources on getting traction among a small number of people in the early majority. Remember the Smarter, Cleaner, Stronger campaign? The singular focus there was on a small subset of the business sector (the business columnists on editorial boards) in each state. We hoped from there to go to businesspeople, and from those to senators.

The second approach is to build the early adopter base large enough that it tips over into the early majority through sheer numbers. To do that, Big Think would have had to become something like a membership organization, or at least to spend significant time and energy getting, keeping, and growing a base of people who promoted its agenda.

Figure 12.2 suggests the kinds of targets you will be engaging based on where in the adoption cycle (from early adopters to laggards) your innovation is aiming. Your hypotheses about growth should reflect the type you've chosen with respect to your targets.

If your innovation truly frames something new, you can expect rapid growth among early adopters but slow growth in the mainstream until you've "crossed over." For Big Think, this looked like a lot of press for its ideas in alternative media with much slower adoption by mainstream media outlets. Its hypotheses about expanding its base needed to be clear about defining the numerical goals it planned on hitting among early adopters, distinct from those targeting mainstream media and funders. The rates would be quite different.

If, on the other hand, you're fortifying and amplifying, then you're seeking to grow your innovation within an existing base of targets who already understand the problem and solution. In that situation, you might hypothesize linear growth within the existing mainstream population. For example, the National Museum for the American Indian tapped existing museum-goers and aimed to capture a linearly growing percentage of visitors to the Washington museum scene.

Overall, remember your lean roots and build an organization that has an eye for hypotheses and data that can confirm or reject your ideas about what will work organizationally to increase your impact over the long term.

Organizational Development and Management: Forming Mission-Driven Departments

The second part of institutionalization is determining the optimal organizational structure for your innovation's growth. This structure can be stand-alone, if your innovation started on its own, independent of other entities, but the structure can be within an existing organization if the innovation was incubated within one. The structure should flow from a mission that's emerged from all the steps you've taken to date and then embed key elements of that mission in each of the structure's components or pieces.

Mission

You already understand your mission. Until this stage, it has been a concise summary of the problem you identified and the solution you developed. Remember that you've gotten this far because you've stayed focused, you've tested your ideas with lots of people in real-world settings, and you've shown that you've got an innovation that works.

For far too many in the social sector, developing an organizational mission (or purpose) feels like a difficult, conflict-laden task. In the vast majority of cases, by the time your team and your board are assembled in one place to determine a mission, it's because you all fundamentally agree on a common mission already. (Real disagreements typically stem not from how you've defined the mission, but from the nitty-gritty details of how to

Figure 12.3 Mission's Role in Structure

allocate funding, what do to first, in what time frame, with which partners, and so forth.)

Remember: Your mission is already a concise summary of your problem/solution pair. To grow your organization, you can add to the mission some of the other operational hypotheses you've proven, including the activities that represent your growth hypothesis and key metrics generated from the validation and creation phases. Not all of these need to make it into the outward-facing mission statement, but they should be well explained in the mission statement used day to day in operating the organization and, ideally, in communicating to your funders.

The fleshed-out, full mission statement should still be concise, but also detailed enough that new employees can read it and know what they are there to do. Table 12.1 shows some samples.

Departments

Your operational mission should be the basis for an organizational structure to grow your innovation to full scale. In the validation and creation phases you built a repeatable and scalable process that built your innovation. Now is the time to embody that process within departments.

The kind of departments you form will depend on the nature of your innovation as well as what function and position you've adopted. Group the activities from your overall mission statement (derived from your experiences in the prior phases). Your functional position (Norms/Behaviors, Laws/Policies, Social and Physical Products and Services/Institutions) should guide this choice, since different types of organizational functions require different types of departments and employees.

Each department in turn has its own mission statement that specifies its purpose, activities, and metrics. These statements are far from generic but must depend instead on the specific learning

Table 12.1 Activities Linked to Missions

Functional Model \ Mission Element	Change Norms and Behaviors	Change Laws and Policies	Build Social and Physical Products, Services, and Institutions
Sample Organization	Catalog Choice	Smarter, Cleaner, Stronger	National Museum of the American Indian
Purpose ("What are we changing in the world?")	Stop junk mail for good	Get four more Senate votes for climate legislation	Advance knowledge and understanding of the Native culture of the Americas
Activity ("What do we do?")	Enroll customers Engage catalog companies Drive zero waste programs in communities Raise money to support operations	Support climate advocacy and labor groups Engage editorial boards Engage local businesses and labor Brief senators Report to climate change groups	Welcome visitors Partner with Native people and others Support the continuance of culture, traditional values, and transitions in contemporary Native life Raise money from donors and governments
Metrics ("How do we measure success?")	Acquire 15,000 new consumers per month Enroll 75% of top catalog mailing companies Achieve break-even through member fees Provide living wage and full benefits to employees	Brief editorial of major newspaper in each state of swing-vote senators and place news story Brief senior staff of senators' offices Enroll at least three corporate partners per state	Have highest attendance in Smithsonian family of cultural institutions Manage access to collection and acquisition process with 30-day or less backlog 15% of expenses covered from grants

you've amassed to date about the optimal organizational types for your innovation and where you are with respect to your targets. *Framing* innovations need to focus a lot on explaining the innovation to populations that may never have seen anything like it and convincing a smaller number of early adopters. *Fortifying/amplifying* innovations, on the other hand, will probably focus on reaching as many people as possible with an innovation that already fits their worldview.

One of the most critical tasks of the institutionalization phase is to continue to monitor your relationship to your targets along the lines you tested in the creation phase. How big is the gap between the people your innovation is reaching today (early adopters) and the early majority beneficiaries? If you are driving an innovation that fits into how people understand the world today, you'll probably want to start scaling. If, on the other hand, you're trying something pretty new (like putting homeless people into permanent houses), your energy will focus less on sheer numbers and more on building a loyal, early base of people who "get" your solution and can help it spread.

As important as the departments you build in this phase are the people you fill them with.

The Right People for the Right Jobs

Hiring the team that will take your innovation to scale is probably the single most important activity you will undertake from here on out. Your success will very likely depend on two factors: the extent to which you've structured the jobs in your organization to meet the mission and the quality and "fit" of the people you hire for those jobs.

Carefully consider the positions you are trying to fill so that they are related to the organization's overall type. There is a big difference between a fundraising director for a startup with a framing position (pushing an idea that's new to the world) and one for a startup that's seeking to convert existing members of a parent organization to a new way of seeing a similar issue. Match the experience to your organization type and the jobs that need to be done to fulfill the mission.

The final key to institutionalizing your innovation is to build creativity and innovation itself into the organization.

A Lasting Culture of Innovation

Remember how the social sector is the sector in which we so often cannot afford to fail? The problems we address aren't always easy to solve, but they often require us to try no matter what. This moral imperative is a remarkable source of innovation in our sector, as well as a remarkable source of the diversity of ideas people have about how to solve problems.

Rather than try to catalog all the paths to innovation, this section focuses on the three meta-components to creating a culture of innovation: innovation accounting, decentralized leadership, and mission clarity.

Innovation Accounting

We discussed innovation accounting in the discovery phase as a way to husband resources. By accelerating the speed of hypothesis testing and decreasing its cost, a startup nonprofit or government project can buy time for more pivots, for more honing of the solution to make it truly game-changing.

Innovation accounting is equally important as your solution gets embedded in a larger, well-established organization. What systems can you put in place that keep you and your team abreast of new developments among your targets, your supporters, key allies? What is an appropriate, ongoing measure of innovative activity?

Many elements of lean practice originated in Japan's automobile industry, but the recent rise of principles of lean startup owes at least as much to the success it's had among software startup companies. While larger companies like General Electric and Intuit are starting to follow suit, not many mature (or at least middle-aged) social sector organizations have adopted lean practices at scale.

Good innovation accounting practices have one thing in common: *they focus on improving rates, not on increasing absolute numbers.* In the discovery phase, the innovation metric was not the number of total tests run, but rather the *rate* at which the number of tests was increasing. The activities of a specific department may well be measured by "making the numbers"—achieving key numerical outcomes. But the measure of innovation within departments should be the rate at which the targets themselves are improving. If the department isn't innovating, it's not the end of the world—it will still be reaching great penetration in its target populations. Sooner or later, however, the department will run into a challenge or a ceiling limiting how high it can go.

A department that is achieving *and* innovating will be spending some of its energy on raising its sights to ever higher targets, and the measure of *that* innovation will be a steady or accelerating increase in the targets themselves. Intuit, one of Silicon Valley's most innovative companies, provides a look at this principle in action.

There are not many "grandparent" companies in Silicon Valley, but Intuit would have to be counted among them. Founded in 1983 and facing intense direct competition from Microsoft for most of the 1990s, Intuit has survived and thrived by innovating throughout its history. Intuit manages innovation by having a distinct innovation pipeline, where each product is rated based on where it is on the experiment-versus-institutionalize spectrum (which Intuit calls the Horizon Planning System). Intuit's metrics for innovation follow the rate-of-rates principle. It seeks to drive continuous improvement in two key performance indicators:

1. How many customers are using products that didn't exist three years ago?
2. How much revenue is coming from products that didn't exist three years ago?

As Eric Ries reported in *The Lean Startup*, Intuit was able to shorten the time it took to reach a threshold of $50 million per year in revenue from 5.5 years to less than twelve months. This focus on accelerating the rate of innovation (that is, changing the rate of the rate) is a prime example of true innovation accounting.

Leadership

The practice of the lean startup owes quite a bit to the invention of lean manufacturing in the Japanese auto industry in the 1950s. Faced with US competitors that had seemingly endless access to capital, Toyota had to find a way to be as productive with far less equipment. Toyota realized that it needed to rely on innovation and continuous improvement and turned instead to the wisdom of its workers on the shop floor. The company is largely managed by these principles to this day.

For innovation to take root in social sector organizations, there needs to be a similar commitment to decentralized learning and leadership. The entire customer development cycle is based on the learning achieved through direct contact with targets and beneficiaries of social sector innovation. Leadership must emanate up from that customer-centric view, from the ground up, and every team member must understand and be attuned to the broader mission.

Innovation is born from a leadership structure that recognizes that the data for innovation relies on the people you serve / customers, and that every customer-facing employee is therefore leading innovation for the organization. By being clear on the mission and key activities, organizations can empower their own people to accelerate innovation.

Mission Clarity and Transparency

Earlier in this chapter we discussed how critical it is to develop a mission statement that clearly embodies what the organization is about. For innovation's sake, the important thing is how the organization drives clarity and transparency in its practice.

Clarity and transparency of the mission is critical for at least three reasons. First, innovation needs to be part of each employee's job, and each employee needs to own the overall mission to be able to contribute to its improvement. Second, true mission transparency keeps different departments in communication and allows cross-organizational innovation. This transparency is particularly important, for example, in fundraising. Imagine, a year out, that a set of grant-makers shifts priorities and reduces the overall funding available to your innovation.

This is *not* the fundraising department's fault, so while that department has to figure out some alternatives, the operational side of the organization must adjust its expenses downward. There may be departmental separation, but the organization as a whole has to innovate its way out of the funding crunch and will be far more likely to do that if the mission is understood fully as being achieved across departments. Finally, mission clarity and transparency are part and parcel of having crisp metrics that help people understand their goals and excel beyond them.

Innovating within an Existing Organization

Can established, mature organizations use lean startup techniques? This book was written for innovators both inside and outside traditional social sector organizations, but some key issues do arise when you're trying to run lean within a mature enterprise.

There *are* major operational differences between developing an innovation and operating an institutionalized program or service. Figure 12.1 showed how the core energy of more mature organizations is focused less on development/experimentation and more on mission and, eventually, process. Innovation is always valuable, but there are legitimate reasons to be nervous if that innovation has to operate side by side with mature, well-established departments and service delivery units. Some examples:

- A fundraising department experimenting with the shift from direct mail to online giving may worry about disrupting existing fundraising channels and reducing overall revenue.
- A hospital experimenting with placing outpatient clinics closer to residential areas may legitimately worry that having fewer intakes at the main hospital may lead to lower core revenue.
- An environmental organization may worry about confusing its constituents if it shifts its campaigns against pollution from a health focus to an economic focus.

These examples and countless others illustrate the need to experiment with evolving the mainstream organization's approach for greater success (or to respond to changing conditions) while preserving its present, proven performance. The key is to recognize both the need to constantly innovate and the legitimacy of protecting the status quo. If you can do that, it becomes a lot easier to keep the overall organization fresh while minimally threatening the stability of its existing operations.

There are a few ingredients to fostering a rich innovation environment within a more mature organization. First, the leadership and as much of the rest of the organization as possible need to explicitly recognize that failure is intrinsic to the parts of the organization that are doing the lean startup and developing innovative initiatives. Without a tolerance for failure (which in the mature parts of the organization would be a signal that things were going quite wrong), the innovation team won't even get off the ground. Leadership needs to decouple traditional mission and process metrics to focus on the learning that the innovation team is meant to generate. Wherever possible, this acceptance of failure must also be communicated to donors, grantors, and other funders.

Another key ingredient is increased communication between the innovation units and the rest of the organization. Drawing the whole organization into the failure and successes of those units will maximize acceptance, enable them to share key learning, and ensure that the parent organization is well equipped to deploy the innovations as they mature and become ready for institutionalization.

Finally, mature organizations should consider creating innovation sandboxes—separate departments, sometimes even located offsite, that are free to develop their own culture, staffing, budgeting, and fundraising appropriate to the innovations they are developing in the parent organization's name. A bit of separation and autonomy can insulate the core organization while fostering the experimental context needed to break through to higher levels.

What to Watch Out for Now That You've Made It: Execution and Environmental Risk

You've successfully institutionalized your innovation when you have an operating model that's scaling your impact, you have a mission and an organization that reflects that mission fully, and you've built a culture of innovation to ensure that you continue to expand your impact well into the future. This stage represents a transition from Build-Measure-Learn to driving a clear mission and, eventually, rigorous processes for ongoing results. After surviving the arduous path of customer development, what's left to worry about?

The leaders of any social sector organization will tell you: lots. Running any organization that's trying to drive change into the world is challenging, not least because often a *lot* of change is needed on really pressing problems. As seen through the lens of the lean startup, though, a few big challenges stand out from the host of day-to-day issues.

First, as you may have noted, the institutionalization phase puts less emphasis on agility—there's less "build–measure–learn" and more "build and operate." This is largely because, by the time you've gotten through the creation phase you're armed with proven strategies for delivering your innovation at scale. Even so, the risk remains that you haven't gotten it quite right, or that there is an even better way to drive change, so your entire team needs to be regularly engaged in making sure your organization is positioned for maximum impact.

The risk inherent in *executing* your innovation lies in how you assemble, operate, monitor, and hire into your organization. Pivoting is a lot harder when you're institutionalized, but adjusting missions, department structures, staffing, and metrics all have to be part of driving higher performance in the service of your solution.

The other major risk you face in institutionalization is environmental risk along at least two lines. The first, just outside the formal boundaries of your organization, is a series of stakeholders you don't control. These include board members, funders, competitors, enemies, and key partners. You've engaged some of them as part of the customer development process, but it will be important as you mature to make sure they are part of your ongoing innovation practice. The lean startup radically speeds learning in organizations, and you need to find a way to keep people who aren't involved on a daily basis engaged in this learning. For board members, ensure that they understand not just your mission but the customer development process itself. For your enemies, make sure someone is watching them throughout your organizational development and suggesting ways you can tweak it to continue to drive change despite opposition.

For funders, oversight entities, partners, and others even further outside the organization, you will have to measure how much to share. At this stage, you are through the major pivots so you will be able to present a pretty stable set of goals and metrics to these external constituencies. Your choices will continue to be informed (more than most in the social sector are used to) by the truth that only close contact with customers, targets, and constituents can provide. This ground truth can be a powerful tool for engaging the external constituencies you most need to stay close to, but they need to be with you for the positive as well as the negative surprises that will ensue from your success.

The second environmental risk is simply the broader social, political, and economic context in which your innovation is operating. This context has been a variable throughout the customer development process, and by following that process not only did you take it into account, but you're also far better prepared to continue to respond to changes in your operating environment as they arise. As you institutionalize, your organization must keep on top of these environmental variables and be prepared to take advantage of those that are favorable and adapt to or defend against those that are not.

An Institution

At the outset of this book, we discussed how the world is, in many ways, changing faster than ever before. The social sector is on the front line for the disruptions wrought by change. By reaching the institutionalization phase of customer development, your innovation and your work have made it a better front line.

You started with the courage to make change, and it takes courage to get this far: the courage to listen to data as it crashes into your dreams, the courage to adapt to what very real people—your customers, your partners, your targets, your funders—show you after you show them that initial dream. The courage to go beyond simple numbers and to understand how to bend the curves and shape the rates that can push you to greater impact. The courage to build an institution that follows the formula you discovered, that holds itself accountable for ongoing innovation, *and* that is promoting change for the better in a world that sorely needs it.

Congratulations! You're not a startup anymore.

Conclusion

Lean Change and the Choices Ahead

The practice of the lean startup is barely a decade old, but it is here to stay. As I hope this book has shown, lean represents a radical and alternative path to innovation. Its effectiveness is being proven every day in the private sector as new companies that use lean startup techniques find ways to drive astonishing changes in commerce. More and more nonprofits and government agencies are proving that lean techniques work in the social sector as well.

Its staying power lies as much in its effectiveness as in the ways in which it is born of the defining technologies of our era. While the basic focus on people's experience (customers), experimentation, and speed seems that it could have emerged at any time in the last two hundred years, the effects of cell phones, the Internet, ubiquitous cameras, social networks, and GPS and other new technologies have cemented the lean startup's central role. These technologies, married to the lean approach, produce feedback on your actions and ideas, your products, and your services almost instantly.

At the same time, there an almost universal understanding and even expectation that this kind of rapid feedback *is* being collected and *will* be used. The practice of lean startup is growing quickly because many entrepreneurs in government and nonprofits know they can go test their most basic assumptions quickly and with minimal resources. Their speed, their data, their focus on hypothesis testing—these practices challenge established conventions wherever lean approaches crop up, and most government and philanthropic sources of funding don't yet know what to make of this upstart method of making social change.

The experience of social and private sector entrepreneurs points to numerous choices about how to fulfill the potential of the lean startup. This book was written to help you overcome the central one, which is how to drive far-reaching innovations *while* listening to customers—how to work with the people you seek to serve to develop your vision into a powerful instrument of change. These new ways to innovate will also require choices beyond the specifics of the lean startup approach.

Funding Choices

Institutionally we need to see a shift, mirroring the one happening now in the private sector, in how we fund innovation. Philanthropists and government agencies need to learn how to support lean approaches and how to pivot when necessary. Several government and philanthropic funders have started embodying new models inspired by the lean startup:

- New Media Ventures and the Knight Foundation both have innovation funds specifically geared for rapid prototyped social change.
- The William and Flora Hewlett Foundation has an annual competition for worst grant. This is the equivalent of a venerated Silicon Valley conference entitled FailCon, that celebrates failing fast.

- The David and Lucille Packard Foundation has created an innovation docket focused on climate policy.
- The White House and the General Services Administration have both pioneered innovation incubators within the federal government.
- And there are even micro-philanthropies, like the Pollinator Project and the Awesome Foundation, which each distribute $1,000 grants every day to help support promising new ideas.

Throughout this book we've discussed funders as a customer in the customer development framework, and this viewpoint puts the onus on the entrepreneur to find the solutions that work for funders. If the social sector is to reap the benefits of the lean startup at scale, more funders will have to join the fray. You can stay tuned at www.leanchange.net/funders for news about how grantmakers and government budget makers are engaging lean innovation.

Transition Choices and Cultural Choices

A meta-challenge is how to shift gears from the old Plan–Fund–Do way to the lean startup, particularly when you're trying to drive innovation within an existing organization. In that context, not only do *you* have to be ready for the failures that come with "first contact" with customers, but the organization and your colleagues have to absorb painful new data about whether what they've been doing makes sense or not.

The stability and performance of the mature organization, discussed briefly in the previous chapter, can coexist with new, internal lean experiments if the relationships have been properly thought through. In those contexts, it's important to create "sandboxes" where lean innovation can run free. The teams working within the innovation sandbox can operate in customer development mode, running agile experiments in search of solution and growth models that work. The main body of the institution can carry on, focused on mission and process for service delivery and later strategically incorporating the sandbox learnings as they mature.

Shifting between old and new practices can be difficult, and experience has shown that lean startup practitioners need a community of practice and ongoing dialogue with peers facing similar challenges. There are a number of resources from the for-profit world as well as nascent resources for social sector practitioners, and you can find pointers to these at www.leanchange.net/community.

Lean practice is also about a change in organizational culture, even more so as it applies to the social sector. Who pays and who benefits are complex questions, and much of the compensation is nonmonetary. What we're not earning in hard currency is often more than made up for by the difference we're making in the world and the teams of dedicated people with whom we work.

Think of some of the archetypal teams in the social sector— police officers on patrol, crews in emergency rooms, museum curators, schoolteachers, legislative staffs, sanitation workers, neighborhood organizers, church leaders. The social sector is a relationship-rich world where the work, every day, puts people in service to much more than a bottom line. In such a complex environment, it can feel more comfortable to think of our closest colleagues and our partners as our most important customers. What becomes important is how well we executed on the stuff we already know how to do, and how well we treated each other when we did it.

Nonprofits and government agencies are usually optimizing for mission and process, when innovation calls for the lean, experimental, data-driven approach of customer development. These cultures and values are not at odds. Mission and process optimization aim to consistently deliver a proven innovation. Customer development is about rigorously testing unproven ones.

These two approaches simply serve different purposes in the lifecycle of change-making, and social sector organizations must become bicultural to foster true innovation. They must avoid pitting the experimental, speed-oriented values of the lean startup against those held in the rest of the organization. Until the innovations get to product–market fit, they are simply experiments and not challenges to the status quo. Similarly, the mature parts of a movement or organization need to be open to honestly evaluating new alternatives and to implementing transformative products and services for social good.

Where Do We Go from Here: Commerce or Community?

> Where do we go from here? First, we must massively assert our dignity and worth.
> Martin Luther King, Jr., *August 16, 1967*

One implication of the lean startup, to quote an inventor of the World Wide Web, is that "software is eating the world." The efficiency with which companies can now quantify and meet demand for products using lean techniques is driving a global transformation in almost every business sector. The effects go far beyond bargain prices for consumers. Other impacts include how efficiencies in new product development are driving a crisis in middle-class employment, as well as the ways in which lean startup techniques were behind some of the decisions that overleveraged the housing market and caused the Great Recession of 2008.

The births of both the 20th and 21st centuries were marked by severe social crises, stemming in large measure from employment crises and severe inequality that, in turn, resulted from the concentration of power and wealth that rapid increases in the productivity of commerce engendered. In a nutshell, the unprecedented efficiency in commercial innovation that the lean startup enables is potentially crippling to the way we work and live today. It will fall to the social sector to mitigate the suffering and, ultimately, to find a cure.

If the techniques of the lean startup helped generate this crisis, can they also help fix it?

I believe the answer is a resounding yes. The same method, applied to the social sector, can have even greater power to mobilize people and communities. Where the lean startup for business has been wildly effective at learning about people's commercial needs, the lean startup for social change can do the same for their social and political needs and, in doing so, help us find the ways to bring our commercial system back in line with our broader values and aspirations.

The lean startup for social change is a radical new way to listen to people, whether you call them customers, targets, clients, or constituents, and to make change based on their needs. As such, it is also a force for innovative democratization. Driven by people's lived experience, it offers the best hope to counter a culture that values commercial efficiency at any expense with one that finds the most powerful social innovations and builds lasting change for the better.

Resources: Sample Lean Change Canvases

The Lean Change Canvas

Designed for: National Museum of the American Indian
Designed by: Michel Gelobter
May 26, 2014
Iteration v1.1

Partners
-George Heye Collection
-Key Tribal leaders
-New York State Legislature

Key Activities
-Building construction
-Moving and managing the collection
-Repatriating remains
-Museum Exhibits
-Membership
-Research

Key Resources
- Huge legacy collection in NY State
-Strong Congressional support

Value Propositions

(Problems)
- Native American artifacts poorly stored and inaccessible
-National collection housed in isolated New York facility
-New York unwilling to cede control over collection

(Solutions)
-Move collection to new facilities
-Maintain significant presence in New York

Relationships
(Museum visitors)
-Member
-Occasional visitor
-Once-in-a-lifetime visitor

(Researcher)
-Physical repository
-Online repository

(Native communities)
-Expert advice on artifact preservation
-Repository for key cultural artifacts

Channels/Pathways
-New Buildings in New York City and in Washington, D.C.
-Online/Digital Resources

Targets

(Direct)
-Museum-going public
-Researchers
-Native communities looking for a repository for cultural artifacts

(Indirect)

(Funders)
Congress
Smithsonian Trustees
Tribes
Individual Donors

Expense Structure
-Capital expense of building 3 facilities
-Operating expense for 3 facilities
-Support for field presence on tribal lands

Revenue Streams
-Congressional appropriation
-George Heye Trust
-Admission
-Membership dues
-Researcher access fees

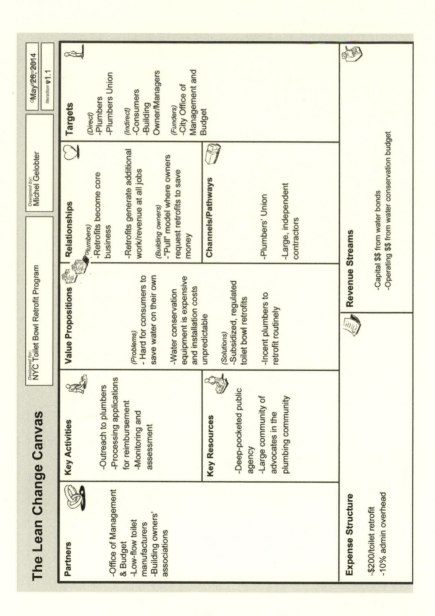

The Lean Change Canvas

NYC Toilet Bowl Retrofit Program

Designed by: Michel Gelobter

©May 26, 2014

Iteration v1.1

Partners

-Office of Management & Budget
-Low-flow toilet manufacturers
-Building owners' associations

Key Activities

-Outreach to plumbers
-Processing applications for reimbursement
-Monitoring and assessment

Key Resources

-Deep-pocketed public agency
-Large community of advocates in the plumbing community

Value Propositions

(Problems)
- Hard for consumers to save water on their own

-Water conservation equipment is expensive and installation costs unpredictable

(Solutions)
-Subsidized, regulated toilet bowl retrofits

-Incent plumbers to retrofit routinely

Relationships

(Plumbers)
-Retrofits become core business

-Retrofits generate additional work/revenue at all jobs

(Building owners)
-"Pull" model where owners request retrofits to save money

Channels/Pathways

-Plumbers' Union

-Large, independent contractors

Targets

(Direct)
-Plumbers
-Plumbers Union

(Indirect)
-Consumers
-Building Owner/Managers

(Funders)
-City Office of Management and Budget

Expense Structure

-$200/toilet retrofit
-10% admin overhead

Revenue Streams

-Capital $$ from water bonds
-Operating $$ from water conservation budget

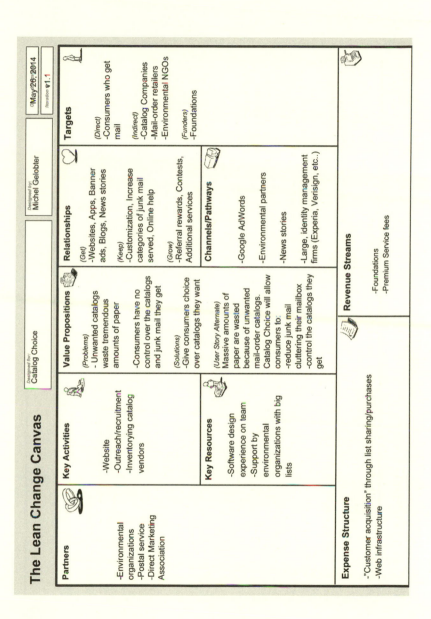

The Lean Change Canvas

Designed for: Catalog Choice
Designed by: Michel Gelobter
©May 26th 2014
Iteration v1.1

Partners

-Environmental organizations
-Postal service
-Direct Marketing Association

Key Activities

-Website
-Outreach/recruitment
-Inventorying catalog vendors

Key Resources

-Software design experience on team
-Support by environmental organizations with big lists

Value Propositions

(Problems)
- Unwanted catalogs waste tremendous amounts of paper

-Consumers have no control over the catalogs and junk mail they get

(Solutions)
-Give consumers choice over catalogs they want

(User Story Alternate)
Massive amounts of paper are wasted because of unwanted mail-order catalogs. Catalog Choice will allow consumers to:
-reduce junk mail cluttering their mailbox
-control the catalogs they get

Relationships

(Get)
-Websites, Apps, Banner ads, Blogs, News stories

(Keep)
-Customization, Increase categories of junk mail served, Online help

(Grow)
-Referral rewards, Contests, Additional services

Channels/Pathways

-Google AdWords

-Environmental partners

-News stories

-Large, identity management firms (Experia, Verisign, etc..)

Targets

(Direct)
-Consumers who get mail

(Indirect)
-Catalog Companies
-Mail-order retailers
-Environmental NGOs

(Funders)
-Foundations

Expense Structure

-"Customer acquisition" through list sharing/purchases
-Web infrastructure

Revenue Streams

-Foundations
-Premium Service fees

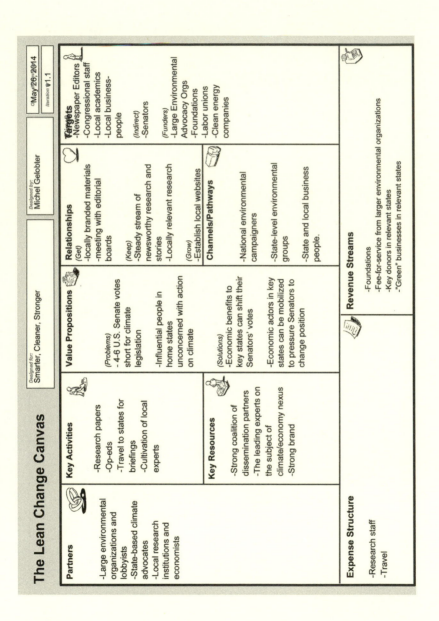

The Lean Change Canvas

Designed for: Smarter, Cleaner, Stronger

Designed by: Michel Gelobter

May 26, 2014

Iteration V1.1

Partners

- Large environmental organizations and lobbyists
- State-based climate advocates
- Local research institutions and economists

Key Activities

- Research papers
- Op-eds
- Travel to states for briefings
- Cultivation of local experts

Key Resources

- Strong coalition of dissemination partners
- The leading experts on the subject of climate/economy nexus
- Strong brand

Value Propositions

(Problems)
- 4-6 U.S. Senate votes short for climate legislation
- Influential people in home states unconcerned with action on climate

(Solutions)
- Economic benefits to key states can shift their Senators' votes
- Economic actors in key states can be mobilized to pressure Senators to change position

Relationships

(Get)
- locally branded materials
- meeting with editorial boards

(Keep)
- Steady stream of newsworthy research and stories
- Locally relevant research

(Grow)
- Establish local websites

Channels/Pathways

- National environmental campaigners
- State-level environmental groups
- State and local business people.

Targets

- Newspaper Editors
- Congressional staff
- Local academics
- Local business-people

(Indirect)
- Senators

(Funders)
- Large Environmental Advocacy Orgs
- Foundations
- Labor unions
- Clean energy companies

Expense Structure

- Research staff
- Travel

Revenue Streams

- Foundations
- Fee-for-service from larger environmental organizations
- Key donors in relevant states
- "Green" businesses in relevant states

Bibliography

Blank, Steven G., and Bob Dorf. *The Startup Owner's Manual: The Step-by-Step Guide for Building a Great Company*. Pescadero, CA: K&S Ranch, 2012.

———. "Why the Lean Startup Changes Everything." *Harvard Business Review*, May 2013, 2–9.

———. *Four Steps to the Epiphany: Successful Strategies for Products That Win*, 2nd edn. Pescadero, CA: K&S Ranch, 2013.

Collins, James C. *Good to Great and the Social Sector*. New York: Harper-Collins, 2005.

Grimm, Kristen. "Just Enough Planning Guide." Planning to Win: The Just Enough Guide for Campaigners, www.planningtowin.org.

Kanczula, Antonia. "Kony 2012 in Numbers." *Guardian*, April 20, 2012, www.theguardian.com/news/datablog/2012/apr/20/kony-2012-facts-numbers?newsfeed=true#zoomed-picture.

Maurya, Ash. *Running Lean: Iterate from Plan A to a Plan That Works*. Sebastopol, CA: O'Reilly, 2012.

Moore, Geoffrey A. *Crossing the Chasm: Marketing and Selling High-Tech Products to Mainstream Customers*. New York: HarperBusiness, 1999.

Osterwalder, Alexander, Yves Pigneur, and Tim Clark. *Business Model Generation: A Handbook for Visionaries, Game Changers, and Challengers*, 1st edn. New York: John Wiley and Sons, 2010.

Ries, Eric. *The Lean Startup: How Today's Entrepreneurs Use Continuous Innovation to Create Radically Successful Businesses*. New York: Crown Business, 2011.

Acknowledgments

This book owes its genesis to the wisdom that has been shared with me by too many people to properly list them all here. In every place I have ever worked, whether not-for-profit, government, or business, some part of our time was spent imagining and trying to make real a better world. And in each place I've been gifted with the wisdom and experience of all of my colleagues. If I have worked with you, next to you, or even against you (think Dick Cheney), thanks.

I could not have written this book without the truly amazing support of the David and Lucille Packard Foundation and the staff in all the different programs there that were interested in innovation and how to bring more of it into their work. Audrey Chang, Chris DeCardy, Alexia Kelly, Carol Larson, Kai Lee, Jamaica Maxwell, and Diana Scearce were my most regular partners in discussion and sources of insight into how philanthropy and lean startups might start to come together. Walt Reid, director of the Conservation and Science Program, gave me the backbone and the support to bring all that I could to the table in service of this book.

The Movement Strategy Center in downtown Oakland housed me as I wrote, but also spiritually grounded me through its commitment to doing right and making a big difference.

Thanks particularly to Philliph Drummond, Taj James, and Lisa McCalla. (And Taj is an encyclopedia of change models.) My editor/publisher at Berrett-Koehler, Steve Piersanti, was on me for years to put more of my words in writing, and he was then patient and strong for the process. Andre Carothers coached me through some big doldrums with great care and thoughtfulness.

Steve Blank really started it all for me, first with his first book *Four Steps to the Epiphany*, and then with his mentorship in my first company and in the finishing of this book. Eric Ries has been a huge role model about how to elegantly prod practitioners, how to make it simple and popular, and how to keep values at the heart of the business of promoting the lean startup. Leah Neaderthal and Leanne Pittsford have been at the forefront of customer development for lean in the social sector, and I owe them a debt for the meetings and the networks that they have assembled over the last couple of years. Christie George, Colin Mutchler, and Rachel Weidinger are real blackbelts out there pushing the boundaries of lean in the social sector, and Amanda Berger, Ludovic Blain, Vivian Chang, David Hodgson, Mimi Ho, and Meena Palaniappan are just some of the people who helped me workshop the concepts and gave me early and helpful feedback.

I can't possibly list all the people in government, grassroots advocacy, academia, the faith world, policy wonk-dom, and business who helped shape this material. Some of my most influential business colleagues were Katherine Brittain, Scott Cook, Gary Dillabaugh, Paul Dixon, John Donohoe, Brian Dooley, Tony Fadell, Chris Farinacci (the da Vinci of marketing), Stephanie Hess, Joanna Hoffman, Mike Johnson, Joe Krasko, Olivier Marie, Brett Newbold, Ray Picard, Ruth Protpakorn, Alain Rossmann, Skip Rudolph, Rupesh Shah, Jonathan Skelding, and Joe Teng. Academic mentors and colleagues who never seem to stop innovating include Bunyan Bryant, Bob Bullard, Carmen Concepcion, Michael Dorsey, Pier Gabrielle Foreman, Ruth Gilmore, Jackie Goldsby, John Holdren, Dan Kammen, Dick Norgaard, Dara ·O'Rourke, Julie Tse, and Beverly Wright. The spiritual teachers who taught me about the inner pivots that keep us all going include Thich Nhat Han, J. Alfred Smith, and Barbara Brown Taylor.

Watching and working with some of the greats in government and politics taught me how much I didn't know about power and its role in shaping the world. Thanks there to Gale Brewer, Shirley Chisholm, Jack Clough, John Dingell, David Dinkins, Mike Finnegan, Dick Frandsen, Patrick Gaspard, Bill Lynch, Ruth Messenger, Basil Patterson, Victor Quintana, Charlie Rangel, Percy Sutton, and Mike Woo.

I have served the Natural Resources Defense Council and CERES as a board member for, cumulatively, over thirty years, but I've been the one learning every step of the way. The extraordinary leadership and staff of these organizations and others I've had the privilege to advise or serve coached me, inspired me, and showed me new ways to get past the dead ends. For that I thank particularly Adam Albright, Frances Beinecke, Paige Brown, Maggie Fox, Peter Goldmark, Michael Green, Paul Hawken, Andrew Hoerner, Rampa Hormel, Michael Klein, Mindy Lubber, and Ansje Miller, but after them the list gets super-long!

The most intense startup I've ever been part of is the environmental justice movement and its global counterpart, the climate justice movement. It's the place where I learned that, when all else fails, even "the stones will cry out." Some of my teachers there include Dana Alston, Ben Chavis, Luke Cole, Cecil Corbin-Mark, Jihan Gearon, Tom Goldtooth, Richard Moore, Peggy Shepard, and Damu Smith, but there are far too many others to name here. First among my teachers across all domains, though, have been the frontline communities I've had the privilege to serve: Williamsburg, the South Bronx, and Harlem in New York; Camden and Newark, New Jersey; Vieques, Puerto Rico; the Sac and Fox Nation and Akwesasne; and so many others. I owe them the lived experience of their innovations for the most basic rights, for their survival, and for their dignity and grace.

My friends' unwavering support and excitement for this project has been revitalizing on every day I was tired or juggling too much: Amanda Berger, Brad Edmondson, David Ellington, Maurice Emsellem, Shiela Hingorani, Rhodessa Jones, Adam and Dorothy Kahane, Miles, Jay Ou, and Nora Pauwels.

For motivating me every day to value her fully, to accept her gifts and her perfection, thanks to our Mother Earth, her trees and mountains, smells and tastes, and animal and vegetable partners in the whole of creation.

I was raised with an ethos of "innovate or die." Another book or two would be necessary to tell about that, but it was always tempered with love within our family, love for each other, and, sometimes even more, love for our community and for making the world a better place. This was a feeling that came from every side and down from on high. Thanks to my grandparents, Norbert and Hela Gelobter and Muriel and Herbert Warren, and to my super-activist parents, Barbara and Ludwig. I'm so glad I have my siblings, David and Lisa and Valerie, to trade notes with and love how, even though we do very different things, they roll like committed and conscientious entrepreneurs wherever they work.

The best for last: three teenagers I lived with while I wrote this book showed me the miracle of invention, of starting up every day. Nathan, Marco, and Troy—you have polished and perfected me, opened me. Thank you for my life.

Index

About the Author

It took Michel about twenty-five years of work on environmental and social justice to realize that his real specialty was startups. His career has moved in seven-year increments through government, academia, advocacy, and, most recently, business. The intense focus on innovation and launching startups in this last phase brought him to the realization that, 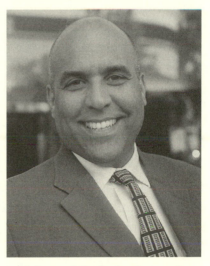 in each of his prior incarnations, his work had also been about bringing new things to light in the world.

He was raised in a community of innovators—community activists who reformed Democratic machine politics in New York City and helped make Shirley Chisholm the first black person to run for president of the United States. As a graduate student at Berkeley, Michel wrote the first doctoral dissertation in the field of environmental justice and co-taught the first class at any university in the field as well.

He returned to political work after graduate school, working for Rep. John Dingell's Energy and Commerce Committee, and later moved back to New York to serve as Mayor Dinkins's Director of Environmental Quality. As assistant commissioner to the city's $2 billion a year water and environmental agency, he started demand-side and watershed management for the city's water system, and these programs have reduced demand in the city by almost 25 percent.

He was invited by Columbia University's School of International and Public Affairs to start its environmental policy program. During this period he co-founded a number of local and regional environmental justice organizations and water and oceans organizations, as well as the country's first multistate community-based research consortium at Rutgers University in New Jersey.

Michel moved back to Berkeley in 2001 to teach and to lead Redefining Progress, at the time the country's only national sustainability policy institute. He and the team there pioneered new ways of thinking about climate policy primarily as economic and employment policy. Under a federal government that was committed to inaction on climate change, Redefining Progress helped California and nine northeastern states adopt legislation that today raises over $3 billion a year in revenue from fees on carbon emissions.

Michel focused next on addressing the new imperative for sustainability in the business world. He started as a software entrepreneur in 2007, launching a social venture called Cooler that aims to activate consumers to make better choices. He subsequently joined a Kleiner-Perkins portfolio company, Hara, that became the leading provider of enterprise-scale environmental management software and put over a million buildings' worth of energy data in the cloud as a co-founder of BuildingEnergy.com.

Most recently, Michel worked as a Senior Fellow with the David and Lucille Packard Foundation to help develop new approaches to innovation in global climate philanthropy. In this role he designed experiments in Turkey, Australia, and Indonesia and helped to develop a prize-winning platform specific to climate challenges.

Berrett–Koehler
Publishers

Berrett-Koehler is an independent publisher dedicated to an ambitious mission: *connecting people and ideas to create a world that works for all.*

We believe that to truly create a better world, action is needed at all levels—individual, organizational, and societal. At the individual level, our publications help people align their lives with their values and with their aspirations for a better world. At the organizational level, our publications promote progressive leadership and management practices, socially responsible approaches to business, and humane and effective organizations. At the societal level, our publications advance social and economic justice, shared prosperity, sustainability, and new solutions to national and global issues.

A major theme of our publications is "Opening Up New Space." Berrett-Koehler titles challenge conventional thinking, introduce new ideas, and foster positive change. Their common quest is changing the underlying beliefs, mindsets, institutions, and structures that keep generating the same cycles of problems, no matter who our leaders are or what improvement programs we adopt.

We strive to practice what we preach—to operate our publishing company in line with the ideas in our books. At the core of our approach is stewardship, which we define as a deep sense of responsibility to administer the company for the benefit of all of our "stakeholder" groups: authors, customers, employees, investors, service providers, and the communities and environment around us.

We are grateful to the thousands of readers, authors, and other friends of the company who consider themselves to be part of the "BK Community." We hope that you, too, will join us in our mission.

A BK Currents Book

This book is part of our BK Currents series. BK Currents books advance social and economic justice by exploring the critical intersections between business and society. Offering a unique combination of thoughtful analysis and progressive alternatives, BK Currents books promote positive change at the national and global levels. To find out more, visit **www.bkconnection.com**.

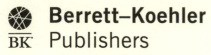

Berrett–Koehler
Publishers

Connecting people and ideas
to create a world that works for all

Dear Reader,

Thank you for picking up this book and joining our worldwide community of Berrett-Koehler readers. We share ideas that bring positive change into people's lives, organizations, and society.

To welcome you, we'd like to offer you a free e-book. You can pick from among twelve of our bestselling books by entering the promotional code **BKP92E** here: http://www.bkconnection.com/welcome.

When you claim your free e-book, we'll also send you a copy of our e-newsletter, the *BK Communiqué*. Although you're free to unsubscribe, there are many benefits to sticking around. In every issue of our newsletter you'll find

• A free e-book
• Tips from famous authors
• Discounts on spotlight titles
• Hilarious insider publishing news
• A chance to win a prize for answering a riddle

Best of all, our readers tell us, "Your newsletter is the only one I actually read." So claim your gift today, and please stay in touch!

Sincerely,

Charlotte Ashlock
Steward of the BK Website

Questions? Comments? Contact me at bkcommunity@bkpub.com.

MIX
From responsible
sources
FSC® C113845

Certified

Corporation
bcorporation.net